FULL CIRCLE

NINETY YEARS OF SERVICE
IN THE MAIN READING ROOM

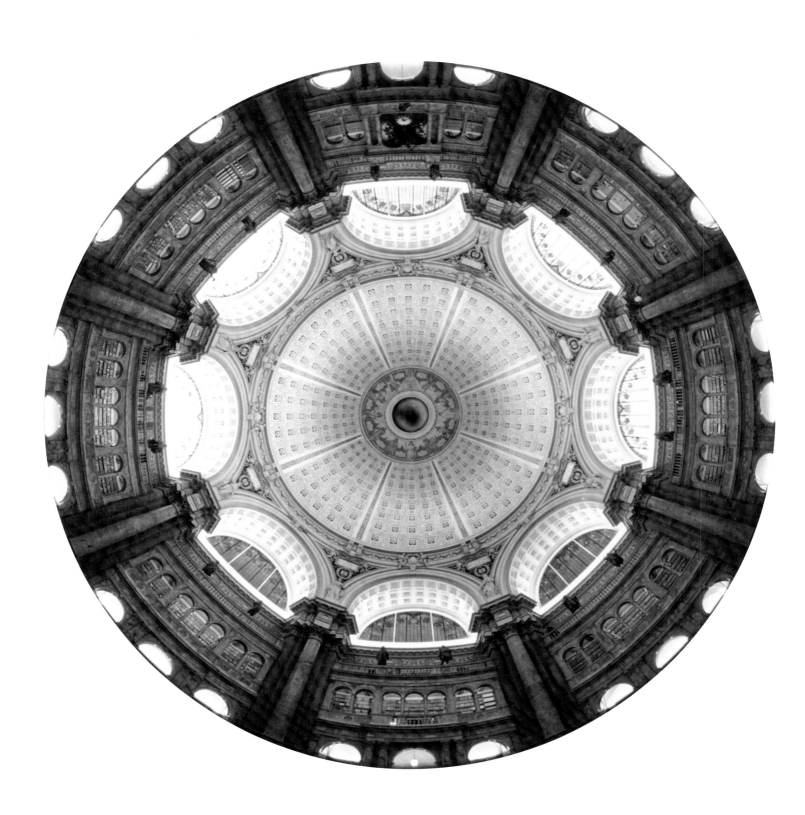

FULL CIRCLE

NINETY YEARS OF SERVICE
IN THE MAIN READING ROOM

BY JOSEPHUS NELSON AND JUDITH FARLEY

GENERAL READING ROOMS DIVISION

LIBRARY OF CONGRESS · WASHINGTON · 1991

A publication of the Center for the Book in the Library of Congress, made possible by private contributions to the center.

Library of Congress Cataloging-in-Publication Data

Nelson, Josephus.
    Full Circle: ninety years of service in the Main Reading Room / by Josephus Nelson and Judith Farley.
      p.   cm.
    Includes bibliographical references (p.   ).
    ISBN 0-8444-0726-7
    ——— ——— Copy 3 Z663 .F85 1991
    1. Library of Congress — History. 2. Reference services (Libraries) — Washington (D.C.) — History — 20th century. 3. Libraries, National — United States — History — 20th century. 4. Reading rooms — Washington (D.C.) — History — 20th century.
I. Farley, Judith. II. Title.
Z733.U6N37 1991   91-14571
027.573 — dc20   CIP

Cover: A watercolor rendering for the marblework in the Main Reading Room by Howard Sill, 1893. Architecture, Design, and Engineering Collections, Prints and Photographs Division.

Frontispiece: The interior of the dome. LC-USP6-4730-MI

Note on the illustrations: Negative numbers given in the illustration captions may be used to order copies from the Photoduplication Service, Library of Congress.

∞ The paper in this publication meets the requirements for permanence established by the American National Standard for Information Science "Permanence of Paper for Printed Library Materials," ANSI Z39.48-1984.

Book design by Robert Wiser, Meadows & Wiser, Washington, D.C.

For sale by the Superintendent of Documents, U.S. Government Printing Office, Washington, D.C. 20402.

CONTENTS

The Thomas Jefferson Building of the Library of Congress, opened to the public in 1897, is a powerful symbol of learning and democracy. It also is an inspired union of architecture, culture, and the arts. As the building's centennial approaches, its art and architecture are receiving renewed attention from scholars and historians. It is appropriate that this book, the first of several publications about the Library planned for this anniversary decade, tells the story of public service in the Jefferson Building's most important place and symbol: the Main Reading Room. Moreover, its authors are staff members who work in the "noble room" and have been inspired by it.

The Center for the Book in the Library of Congress was established in 1977 to stimulate public interest in books, reading, and libraries and to encourage the study of books and print culture. The Library of Congress occupies a unique place in American civilization. So does its Main Reading Room. The Center for the Book is pleased to make an important part of the Library's history available to a wide public.

JOHN Y. COLE
DIRECTOR, THE CENTER FOR THE BOOK

The imagery of the circle is everywhere in the Main Reading Room. From the solid center desk in the middle of the floor to the aspiring rings of the dome, circles predominate. So too between scholar and librarian circles of service rotate daily—the alternation of query and response. From the original opening of the room almost a century ago to the reopening now of this magnificently restored learning center, we have come full circle. As the room opens again to readers and researchers, so will the circle of service assert its traditional place in the Main Reading Room, itself the center of the Thomas Jefferson Building and the primary locus of research in the Library of Congress.

Opened in 1897 to great acclaim, by 1987 the room needed extensive renovation to restore its original beauty and to improve its technological capabilities to meet the needs of scholars in the twenty-first century. In anticipation of the day the Main Reading Room is again ready to greet its admirers, we offer this tribute to the room and its role in the Library, to the staff who animated it and gave it purpose, and to the Librarians of Congress whose leadership nourished it.

The vignettes presented here are freeze-frames of life and work in the Main Reading Room over the years, arranged by administrations of Librarians of Congress to provide context. The Library's manuscript and print archives yielded wonderful treasures: the men and women who wrote the official reports of the Library and the Reference Department did so in eloquent and often elegant prose. Their voices are distinctive, and so we have used their words to tell much of the story.

Through their administrative eyes we learn something about reference guidelines and time limitations, staffing patterns and shortages, reference trends and reader preoccupations, staff qualifications and quality. In the later years we catch a glimpse of the workaday world of the reading room through the eyes of its staff.

The task of gathering the voluminous documentation was shared by Josephus Nelson, Judith Farley, Mary Catherine Ammen, and Lynn Pedigo, all reference specialists in the current Main Reading Room Section of the General Reading Rooms Division. The joyful labor of deciding what should be included and what must be, with reluctance, set aside fell to Mr. Nelson and Ms. Farley, as did the writing of this history. All the participants have asked me to extend their thanks to their section head and assistant section head, Victoria C. Hill and Larry M. Boyer, for their encouragement and assistance, to Marguerite Bloxom, bibliographic specialist, for her careful and graceful editing, to John Knowlton, Manuscript Division, and the staff of the Manuscript Reading Room, who so effectively opened the resources of the Library of Congress Archives to us, and to Evelyn Sinclair of the Publishing Office whose deft touch ensured speedy publication of this work. It is my pleasure to do so.

"Notes toward a history" would be a truer description of this work than "a history" — to do full justice to the Main Reading Room must be the task of a library historian. Until the full story is told, however, we hope that our word pictures will serve as a happy remembrance of the reopening of the Main Reading Room.

SUZANNE E. THORIN
CHIEF, GENERAL READING ROOMS DIVISION

T he Library of Congress existed for almost a hundred years before its stately quarters and magnificent reading room were built. The first appropriation for its support was passed in 1800, and the first catalog describing its holdings (with volumes listed according to size) was issued in 1802. Housed in a portion of the U.S. Capitol building the library then consisted of "212 folios, 164 quartos, 581 octavos, 7 duodecimos, and 9 maps" (**20** p. 2).★

British troops destroyed the entire collection by fire in the War of 1812. To reseed the collection Thomas Jefferson offered to sell, at cost, much of his personal library, 6,487 volumes. From that nucleus the library grew steadily. Under the influence of Librarian Ainsworth Rand Spofford, appointed by President Lincoln in 1864, the copyright law was revised to ensure that two copies of every book copyrighted would be deposited in the Library of Congress. From that time the growth of its holdings has continued unchecked.

A new building to house the burgeoning collections was eight years in construction from its congressional approval in 1889 to its occupation in 1897. At the center of the new building was the reading room, whose ceiling telescoped into the very tip of the dome. The room, replete with statuary, gilded rosettes, railings, arches, and stained glass, provided a visual feast for weary readers whose eyes were distracted upward from their books.

But the Main Reading Room is more than an architectural triumph. It is the living center of the Library, the hall where searchers gather to pursue the knowledge concealed in the volumes of its holdings. Here their search is mediated by reference librarians (formerly the library assistants) who are the human presence of the Library. Without aid potential readers might turn away in dismay, unable to penetrate the maze of the Library's shelves and cases. *Full Circle*, while it touches many aspects of the Library of Congress and its great reading room, is primarily the story of these librarians, and their struggles and triumphs.

★Throughout the text information about sources will be presented in parenthetical notes. The bold number identifies the source in the Selected List of References, pages 61–62.

BY 1890, THE NEED FOR SPACE IN THE LIBRARY'S QUARTERS IN THE CAPITOL WAS
DESPERATE—BOOKS WERE PILED ON TABLES AND MAIL BAGS WERE STORED UNDER THEM.
DAVID HUTCHESON, SEEN STANDING IN THE BACKGROUND AT RIGHT IN THIS
PHOTOGRAPH, WOULD MOVE THANKFULLY INTO THE NEW LIBRARY OF CONGRESS
BUILDING IN 1897 AS THE FIRST SUPERINTENDENT OF THE READING ROOM. LC-USZ62-598

"The great sight of the Library," wrote Paul Angle, is "the very heart of the institution, the reading room. That should be seen from the visitors' gallery and at night. Even though one stands at a back-breaking height above the floor, the dome, lined with book stacks and strung with lights, reaches far above; while below, the dark surfaces of hundreds of desks, in concentric broken circles, gleam with the shaded lights of intent readers. Even the brashest tourist speaks in a whisper. What goes on here, he perceives instinctively, matches the majesty of the surroundings" (**2** p. 4).

FROM THE OPENING DAY: EVOLUTION OF POLICY

A *Washington Post* reporter, describing the November 1, 1897, opening of the new Library of Congress building, wrote "The first day of the Library's public service passed off without incident" (Nov. 2, p. 11). On that first day rain-spattered Library visitors were permitted to enter the building at 8:30 A.M. A watchman, stationed outside the Main Reading Room, carefully screened them, admitting to this room only potential readers, at 9:00 A.M. Upon entering the reading room readers found a waiting and mindful staff, volumes of reference books lining the walls, and a room richly decorated in gleaming wood and sumptuous marble. Hugh Alexander Morrison and John Graham Morrison (not related but both assistants to the superintendent of the reading room), and Willard Moore were positioned at the large circular service desk (the superintendent and his staff were expected to preside over this central point in the room). Surrounding the desk, and taking the place of the first row of seats, were shelves containing a selection of books for ready reference. A small catalog held pride of place inside the desk, and a plentiful supply of tickets (each had a space for an author's name, a book title, and a reader's name) were available for those wishing to order books.

Mr. Vale, private secretary to Rhode Island's Senator Wetmore, requested the first book, but David Hutcheson, superintendent of the reading room, had to tell him with some chagrin that the Library of Congress had not yet received *Roger Williams' Year Book*. Department of Agriculture staff member Dr. Max West, second in line, quickly received Martha Lamb's *History of New York*, and a woman behind him received *Lady Eastlake's Memoirs*.

Service proceeded apace, and at the end of the day John Russell Young, Librarian of Congress, gave credence to the *Washington Post* reporter's comment by declaring that he was well pleased with the book deliveries and the "manner in which the crowds of readers were handled by the attendants." Opening day reader assistance prefigured the attitude toward service that reading room staff would take in the coming years.

Those years would be shaped by the administrations of two men, John Russell Young and Herbert Putnam. Young, who served as Librarian of Congress from 1897 to 1899, was later termed the "Great Beginner," for his short tenure fairly bristled with "firsts." He was the first Librarian

to administer the Library under its new charter, first who would not describe himself nor his office as merely "the organ of the Joint Committee," first to differentiate the collections by form, first to effect the staff organization which Congress had provided, first to preside over the

ON OPENING DAY, NOVEMBER 2, 1897, THE FIRST BOOK ORDERED AND SUCCESSFULLY
RETRIEVED FOR A READER WAS MARTHA J. LAMB'S *HISTORY OF THE CITY OF NEW YORK*,
VOL. 1 (NEW YORK, A. S. BARNES, 1877), THE COVER OF WHICH IS SHOWN HERE.

Library's own building, first to struggle with a scientific classification, first to install a service for
the blind, first to secure the opportunities which go with evening service, first to receive the
promise of a trust fund, first to express the universal concept, and first to perfect the national
principle (**11** 1946, p. 176).

He was also the first Librarian to preside over the new Jefferson Building, but his occupation of the new Librarian's quarters was brief. It was his immediate successor, Herbert Putnam,
who fully exploited the opportunities the new building offered.

Putnam spoke of himself as having "tended" the Library. During his administration

He saw the Library enlarge: a stack for the southeast courtyard, a stack for the northeast courtyard, an auditorium, a pavilion, the eastern extension, the functional Annex. He worked and
watched as the manuscript collections became the greatest body in existence of research materials for the study of the American past—as the music collections attained preeminence—as the
map collections were acknowledged to be unparalleled. . . . It was his card catalog which out-
grew that cabinet within the central desk, was removed to a sector in the reading room, and
thence expanded into adjoining quarters. . . (**21** p. 40).

The new and spacious Main Reading Room offered Library administrators new scope for
increased personal assistance. Although the nineteenth-century Librarians of Congress had
supported improved service to readers, they had been hindered by a small staff and limited

THE MAIN READING ROOM IN 1898, WITH GRACEFUL TABLE LAMPS AND STAR-SHAPED
CLUSTERS OF LIGHTS IN THE BALCONIES. LC-USZ62-47260

space. John Russell Young recognized the importance of aiding researchers as well as members of Congress. In his 1898 annual report he wrote: "The Librarian is glad to note that the Library is becoming, as it were, a bureau of information, consulted by people from all sections. Twenty years ago, and as a rule, the Library was sought for a specific book; today applicants ask advice as to reading, or request special information. It is the policy of the Library to encourage this spirit of inquiry." It was left to Herbert Putnam, eighth Librarian of Congress, and to the Main Reading Room superintendents to define reading room reference service for the next forty years.

A reference service policy slowly evolved under Putnam and his appointed supervisors. Putnam's view, in some degree, is expressed in an 1899 memorandum to Charles Hastings. He explained that the reading room was supervised by a "trained librarian, who with several assistants, is prepared to answer questions as to the best literature on any topic," and to do so "without limit as to time except so far as governed by the exigencies of the service" (**12** fiche 2-8-5). In his 1901 *Report of the Librarian of Congress* he also stressed that "The Main Reading Room is usually the point first approached by an inquirer. It is the duty of the desk attendants to place at his disposal such information as they have" (**11** 1901, p. 244).

William Warner Bishop, Putnam's second appointee to the superintendency of the Main Reading Room, helped in the fine tuning of Library policy. His service philosophy was set out in a series of articles. Two such were "Amount of Help to Be Given to Readers," and "The Theory of Reference Work." In both Bishop took a measured approach. Readers should be helped as much as possible but the librarians must remember that they should guide only, never actually do the work for the reader.

By 1939 the Library's policy had been determined. It had been decided that assiduous but balanced attention would be the hallmark of Main Reading Room reference service. The 1939 *Information for Readers in the Reading Room* contains a firm statement of policy:

> Persons in search of information on particular topics, especially if it be a small item will frequently find what they desire to know in some of the books in the reference collections. The assistants at the reference desk will gladly point out the location of appropriate reference books, and so far as is compatible with the needs of others, aid a reader in securing information. They will always endeavor to be of aid to him, and whenever necessary the problem will be placed before other members of the Library staff or an appropriate division of the Library, or in certain cases referred to our experienced consultants. The Library cannot, however, undertake to conduct research for readers, but must content itself with suggesting material that may bear on the subject (p. 1–2).

THE LIBRARY STAFF: FORGING A TRADITION OF EXCELLENCE

Librarian Putnam chose experienced people to implement the service-oriented program in the Main Reading Room and its dependencies. It fell to the reading room superintendent to supervise assistants and manipulate policy. In the early years those chosen for the position were men of education and talent, many of whom went on to illustrious positions in library work.

David Hutcheson entered the Library of Congress in 1874, rising to the position of principal assistant to Mr. Spofford, before being appointed reading room superintendent in 1897. Hutcheson was praised for management skill: "he has shown executive capacity, courtesy, and tact, and he is especially fitted for the part" (*Library Journal,* August 1897, p. 414), and he was lauded for his knowledge and public service spirit: "his own encyclopedic store of information . . . and intimate knowledge of books in general and the contents of the Library of

Congress in particular, have always been placed freely at the service of any inquirer" (*Library Quarterly*, September 1907, p. 421).

William Warner Bishop, his successor in 1907, and one of the "scholar-librarians," was a University of Michigan graduate, a classicist, and linguist. Before coming to the Library of Congress he had directed reference and cataloging at Princeton. "To the job itself Bishop brought organization & systematization both of which he developed to a high degree." (**16** p. 347). Bishop later wrote of his experience: "The Reading Room post was not easy to fill. Indeed it taxed my powers to the utmost . . . But it was magnificent training" (**3** p. 16). From the Library of Congress Bishop returned to Michigan, where he became director of the university's library system.

Frederick W. Ashley, the first of the reading room superintendents to have been graduated from a library school, served from 1915 until 1926. Trained at New York State Library, Ashley was touted as a resourceful and learned executive. Within the Library of Congress he advanced to become Chief Assistant Librarian, a post he held until 1936.

Martin Arnold Roberts, a longtime Library administrator, was appointed in 1927 and served as superintendent until 1937. "Those with whom he was intimately associated speak of him as 'a man of unremitting and self-sacrificing industry'" (**10** memo, June 16, 1940).

David Chambers Mearns, appointed in 1938, and author of *The Story Up to Now: The Library of Congress, 1800–1946*, started his career "sorting books by size." After a brief interval as an "index-finger typist" he began his noted service in the Main Reading Room. Archibald MacLeish said that Mearns was "the rarest treasure in the Library of Congress," and Luther Evans told him: "You were for me more the embodiment of the Library of Congress than any other person, perhaps because you loved it most"(**13** December 21, 1967, p. 840–841).

EXPERT WAITERS ON THE PUBLIC

To the junior staff, the assistants at the center desk, came the frontline duties of carrying out policy when meeting reader requests. Personnel hired for these positions were expected to have broad backgrounds of education and experience. Not only were strong educational credentials required, but such personal attributes as "good manners, tact, patience, and a good memory" (**10** memo, February 26, 1900) were also emphasized. Gender and race were in some cases specified. Hutcheson, in announcing an assistant position, noted: "For this place a young man preferred as it requires constant activity" (**10** memo, May 29, 1899). In describing a position in the Senate Reading Room, he wrote: "An active colored or white man with good manners and a good education" is needed (**10** memo, May 31, 1899).

Depending on their qualifications and experience, prospective reading room assistants were paid, in 1899, salaries ranging from $720 to $1,200 a year. Joseph Schneider, who had a reading knowledge of four languages, a teachers' degree from the Academy of Paris, and six years experience as assistant librarian at Georgetown College (Washington, D.C.), was appointed at $720 a year. Philip DeWitt Phair, fluent in Latin, French, and German, graduate of Harvard (M.A.), instructor in history and political science at Hartford's Trinity College, and a sometime assistant librarian at Trinity's library, secured a $900 appointment. (Administrators believed that Phair's history and political science background would make him especially effective in answering congressional requests.) Those applicants meriting the $1,200 appointment needed not only a college degree and language skills, but "a wide acquaintance with literature, especially of the literature of the United States and of modern Europe. Fair knowledge of history and geography, and some knowledge of the literature of the various sciences. Experience in a reference, or other large, library giving a knowledge of the sources of information, such as works of ref-

THE GREAT BRONZE DOORS OF THE THOMAS JEFFERSON BUILDING, REOPENED BY
LIBRARIAN OF CONGRESS DANIEL J. BOORSTIN. PHOTOGRAPHED IN 1898. LC-USZ62-74253

erence, and of the methods of classification and cataloging" was essential (**10** memo, February 26, 1900).

Men and women were employed in the Main Reading Room, but women were hired with some reservations. Some in the library community and in the Library of Congress questioned their aptitude and stamina. Mr. William Fletcher, librarian at Amherst College, said in the 1896 hearings before the Joint Committee on the Library: "I agree with what has been said as to the usefulness and efficiency of women in many library positions, especially in cataloging, and at the counters of free public libraries, where by their superior powers of sympathy, they excel as guides and leaders of the reading of those who resort to them. I should, however, consider it doubtful whether they could satisfactorily be employed as librarians or assistants outside of the cataloging work in the Library of Congress" (Joint Committee hearings, 54th Congress, November 20, 1896). In fact, eight women, according to David Hutcheson's 1898 report, were assigned to the Main Reading Room, but their duties were primarily clerical. None was assigned to the reference desk to "strive to reduce the labor of the reader by hospitality to direct inquiries" (**11** 1901, p. 244). Reference desk work apparently was not one of the "gentle and useful offices suitable for women" (**11** 1897, p. 11).

The Main Reading Room employed African-American staff members too. Paul Laurence Dunbar, the celebrated poet, was assigned there. Having charge of one of the decks, he worked from September 1897 until December 1898. An admirer told of visiting him at the Library of Congress. "Climbing four short flights of stairs in the north stack of the Library, I found my poet, seated . . . at a desk, busily engaged on some special work in connection with his present position" (Dunbar papers, Ohio Historical Society). Dunbar gave poetry recitals, too, in the Pavilion of the Blind.

Daniel Murray, an ardent bibliophile and Dunbar colleague, was also assigned to the reading room. Best known for having assembled a collection of the works of African-American authors—the collection is now in the custody of the Rare Book and Special Collections Division—Murray in 1898 worked "mainly in arranging the Smithsonian collection of publications of scientific societies, and on duty in the stacks" (**10** memo, November 2, 1898). In 1910 he is listed as a reading room assistant. Dunbar and Murray do not constitute a representative sample, but their stories give some sense of the positions available to African Americans.

The reading room assistants had many and varied duties. Stationed at the huge reference desk in the center of the room, they provided direct assistance to readers. "So far as is compatible with the needs of others the assistants at the desk will gladly aid a reader in securing information" (*Information for Readers*, 1914, p. 8).

Telephone reference took place at the desk too—"The telephone was constantly in use in requesting books and information"—The assistants also had also some responsibility for correspondence. "In addition, the reading room handles a considerable volume of reference work by correspondence, preparing typed responses in the form of memoranda for transmission through the Librarian's office" (**3** p. 12). The staff's high competency was shown by the wide-ranging reference questions fielded. Responding to a garbled telephone call, the assistants were able to determine that the caller's request for "Dickinson's Notes" was really a call for Charles Dickens's *American Notes*. Similarly they ascertained that the request for "The Tom Horsement of the Afolca Type" was really a request for *The Four Horsemen of the Apocalypse*.

Circulation and interlibrary loan were also services that the staff carried out in the reading room. "For the reading room division of the Library of Congress is also the principal circulation department of the Library," and "the reading room attends also to the interlibrary loan service to libraries throughout the United States" (**3** p. 12).

Congressional requests were received in the reading room; members of Congress and their staff either visited the desk with requests or sent written ones. "When a member wanted information he usually wrote about it. But when he wanted books, he generally came and got them" (**3** p. 13).

The assistants were also responsible for study desk service. "A limited number of tables are available for the use of authors, scholars and governmental researchers whose requirements for the successful prosecution of their studies are obviously greater than those of casual readers" (**10A** 1922, p. 6). Reading room assistants had responsibility for many services that are now carried out by specialized divisions of the Library of Congress.

Library administrators clearly demarcated the boundaries in which reading room assistants worked. Junior staff members were certainly the first contact for many readers, but they did not have the final word in answering queries. "The Main Reading Room is usually the point first approached by an inquirer. It is the duty of the desk attendants to place at his disposal such information as they have; but it is their paramount duty to see that his inquiry reaches the official or division capable of giving him the fullest and most accurate answer" (**11** 1901, p. 244).

Assistants in other Library divisions served as the reference arbiters. Substantive reference work was handled, initially, by the specialized divisions. Assistants in Manuscripts, Maps and Charts, and the Law Library were looked on as the experts. They used their collections to answer many of the more erudite inquiries.

The Bibliography Division served as the major backup for the Main Reading Room force; in fact, Bibliography became the general reference section of the Library. Assistants in that unit prepared bibliographies and lists and undertook those complicated searches which could not be answered by the reading room assistants. Reading room superintendents encouraged the staff to rely on the assistants in the Bibliography Division for help with the long searches and in-depth responses. "I endeavored to instil into the reading room force the idea that any lengthy inquiry was to be turned over to the Bibliography Division—not always with complete success, it must be admitted, for it is contrary to human nature to give up to another an interesting line of investigation" (**3** p. 7).

PROBLEMS AND PERPLEXITIES

The staff's work was hampered because the Main Reading Room did not have the catalogs and indexes that are today considered standard reference tools. In 1897, for example, there was no complete and current catalog.

> The reading room attendants were primarily dependent on the official catalog kept in boxes without rods under the desk in the reading room, "so that the public can not run away with it." Although generally described as an author catalog, it included some subject entries for biographies of individuals and for histories of families, as well as added entries for joint authors or joint editors as authors. This catalog had been compiled by pasting on cards . . . the entries clipped from the printed author catalog of 1864, the last complete author catalog issued, and from the nine printed supplements subsequently issued. The annual supplements of author entries were discontinued with the eighth, that for the year 1872 issued in 1874. The ninth and last supplement issued, in 1876, covered only the principal accessions of the past three years, 1873–1875; but included a title and subject index, in a single alphabet, at the end of the volume (**19** p. 157–158).

In classifying and cataloging the Library's collections the Cataloging Division made a current catalog a possibility. By 1900 a dictionary catalog containing 90,000 cards had been installed on the floor of the reading room.

A BRILLIANTLY LIT VIEW OF THE MAIN READING ROOM AT NIGHT, SUMMER 1912.

DESK ATTENDANTS AT THE CENTRAL DESK, CA. 1913.
LEFT TO RIGHT: CHARLES W. COLLINS, ERNEST KLETSCH, MAURICE H. AVERY,
AND HUGH A. MORRISON.

The assistants appeared, in the early years of the century, to be very much "book detectives" rather than learned purveyors of information. They spent a good bit of their time solving the very real book service problems readers encountered daily. These problems sprang from working with a collection that had not been completely classified or cataloged. Searching for material, consequently, was neither simple nor straightforward. Management relied on the assistants to find clever ways of making the vast but disorganized collection yield the needed sources. This point is made in a story William Warner Bishop told about John Morrison and Hugh Morrison, two of the most senior assistants. "They had literally grown up in it [i.e., the Library] and had gained invaluable knowledge of its books from living with them and seeing them. Time and time again I have seen them solve bibliographical puzzles which had baffled the best brains of the service, not by their learning but by practical skill in finding books" (**3** p. 11).

This practical skill in finding books involved hard work, but work which generated its own interest. "We were on our feet continuously," explained Verner Clapp. "There was much physical labor involved, going around servicing the pressure tubes for the slips, getting the books off the carriers, locating newspapers, delivering books, giving readers instructions on the use of the catalog . . . going anywhere in the Library to get material or information. It was a leg work job, and it was exciting" (**17** p. 4).

Along with the development of the Main Catalog, the assistants, responding to the growing demands on their time and recognizing the need to "get their house in order," developed reference aids to support Main Reading Room service. Superintendent Hutcheson reported that Hugh Morrison and G. T. Ritchie, another Main Reading Room assistant, were compiling, after hours, a fiction index. This index would help the staff in their search for short stories, novels, and romances.

Verner Clapp, a former reading room assistant, reminisced about such work:

> A principal way to improve reference work was obviously to improve bibliography, and each of us had his private bibliographic project. These not only served to occupy spare time and to motivate browsing that might otherwise have been aimless but also gave prestige. Of course, many collections of useless cards were generated, but some achieved lasting value—there was an index . . . to biographies in local histories, a checklist of American almanacs 1639–1800, a bibliography of Alaska, and the reconstituted inventory of Thomas Jefferson (**4** p. 382).

Despite the apparent good humor of the staff, the Library was not always a happy workplace. The Librarian wrote in the 1913 report, "The resignation of desk attendants is an incessant perplexity to the service." Here he posed a pressing problem: How could the Library recruit and keep talented assistants? The well-qualified men and women hired into the Main Reading Room resigned fairly often because of the Library's low salary scale. They did not want to be "left after years of service to live upon wages that a roustabout would deride." The Library expected them to know the literature of librarianship and other disciplines as well and to respond eagerly and expertly to the many questions of a diverse public. Exacerbating the problem was World War I. Many of the experienced assistants entered the service or took better paying war-related jobs, leaving partly trained successors or raw recruits.

The staff had to cope with other related difficulties. The growth of the collection saw a corresponding increase in readers, a larger catalog, and a need for additional room to house the book overflow. Although there were more readers, desks were removed to make room for the catalog and for the constant shifting of the collection. Given the space squeeze the issue of whether secondary students could use the reading room surfaced. The superintendents hesitated to permit high school students to use the room because they did not want it to become a "children's room" and because desk space was at a premium. By 1935 high school and junior college students were restricted to the use of fifty-five desks. When the fifty-five were filled, others had to wait for vacancies. This unsatisfactory solution would not be improved upon until much later.

The Main Reading Room assistants served a large and demanding constituency. The Congress, of course, ranked first. "Many members of Congress had been in Washington for years, and the reading room force knew them personally and intimately. Some came for their own books and would not even let them be sent home by the Library car. Others always sent their secretaries, and still others, various hangers-on. From "Uncle Joe" Cannon down to the latest arrived member they were in search of reading matter" (**3** p. 13).

Members of the public, either in person or through correspondence, used the Main Reading Room reference service. James Truslow Adams observed: "As one looks down on the general reading room . . . one sees the seats filled with silent readers, old and young, rich and poor, black and white, the executive and the laborer, the general and the private . . . all reading at their own library provided by their own democracy" (**1** p. 415).

A goodly number of scholars visited the room too. In fact the superintendents seemed to take great delight in listing the many scholars of note who used the Main Reading Room. Ashley, in a 1927 interview with Helen Christine Bennett, readily named the many famous men and women who had made the Main Reading Room the base for their research. "*The Founding of New England*, by James Truslow Adams, which won the Pulitzer prize for the most notable contribution in the field of American History made in the year of its publication, was entirely written in the Library. Ida Tarbell worked in the Library on her book on Lincoln; Herbert Quick and Hamlin Garland used the Library a great deal while working on their books. Emerson Hough secured here some of the data for *The Covered Wagon*" (*American Magazine*, vol. 103, February 1927, p. 158).

Some of the Main Reading Room users found the staff and service wanting. In 1898 an anonymous and deeply dissatisfied reader wrote a scathing letter to the editors of New York's *Evening Post* (January 31). According to him the inherent confusion and inefficiency in the reading room was compounded by the lack of a scholarly air.

> There are no end of attendants bustling around the central pulpit-desk, and the automatic delivery tubes keep up a great noise, but somehow the books do not come; or, when they come, they turn out to be volumes that have not been asked for. Conversation on the part of the readers is prohibited, but the crowd of employees and messengers do not scruple to speak as loud as may be, and the women clerks bustle about with rustling skirts and with loud-tapping bootheels on the marble floors. The consumptive coughing of the pneumatic delivery tubes goes on continually, and the whole atmosphere of the nation's library in its gorgeous home is as far from scholarly as can be imagined. The placards "Keep Quiet" are hung at the pulpit-desk, from which comes all the noise! After years of possession there is no card catalogue, and if a book does not chance to be in one of the printed catalogues, readers must depend on the memory of the librarians. Altogether the condition of affairs at the new Library appears to be as unsatisfactory as possible.

This reader not only paints a vivid picture of reading room staff and service, but one which shows the reading room in the worst possible light.

Lyman Beecher Stowe held a different view. Writing in a 1937 issue of the *New York Times Magazine* (June 13) he told a story that illustrates the reference standard which Herbert Putnam set for the Main Reading Room at the beginning of the century.

Not so long ago a student wrote to the superintendent of the reading room at the Library of Congress at Washington to say that he wanted to come to the library and use it for two or three weeks going over material which he needed in connection with his writing and lecturing. He mentioned the subjects he wished to look up. When he reached the library three or four days later he was shown to a little office furnished with chairs, a desk and bookshelves containing the books and magazines which he would be most likely to need. His name was even on the door. During his stay he not only was surrounded with the books and papers he needed but received kind and constant advice of experts as to their use.

Librarian Putnam, writing in the 1914 *Report of the Librarian of Congress*, did not indicate any doubts about the quality of service. He judged that the Library had not only made great progress in organizing its collections but that it surpassed all other American librarians in freely making them available and in interpreting them. "The facilities for access to it, for the prompt and convenient use of it, and for the interpretation of it, within the limitations usual to a library, are as a whole, for the investigator, superior to those of any other American library" (p. 10).

Superintendent Roberts in a 1930 annual report supported Putnam's contention. He noted that the Library in its role as "treasure house of source material of international importance" had to expand and "maintain a new quality of service at the Central Desk and the Reference Section of the Reading Room to meet the necessary requirements" of all those wishing to take advantage of the Library's riches. Percy Scholes, a well-known English musicologist, was equally enthusiastic. In a 1932 letter to the *Sunday Times* (October 23) he compared service at the British Museum with service at the Library of Congress. Finding speedy book service, an easy-to-use catalog, and a readiness to permit scholars to enter the stacks, he concluded: "To use the British Museum intelligently experience is needed, whereas a child can use the Library of Congress."

The growth of the collections, the demands of an "information hungry" public, and the increased competence of the assistants led to an evolution in their work. More and more reading room staff became the chief guides for the reader in the use of the Library. They formed the corps of "expert waiters upon the public." Superintendent Roberts, writing in 1930, rejoiced in this transformation in the character of Main Reading Room reference work:

> The change . . . is plainly indicated by the questions asked and the problems placed before the staff of the reading room by these many investigators. In previous years while occasionally research of considerable importance was undertaken, the accent in a large measure was upon the general. The reading room has now grown into something more important than a place set aside for the perusal of books—it has now become a centre of reference work and research (**11** 1930, p. 8–9).

In *The Future in America*, H. G. Wells, observing the United States of the early twentieth century through somewhat jaundiced eyes, reported his disappointment with the lack of an American intellectual life. He was reassured only when he arrived at the Library of Congress to visit with Librarian Herbert Putnam and a small group of other men.

> I lunched with them at their Round Table, and afterwards Mr. Putnam showed me the Rotunda, [now called the Main Reading Room] quite the most gracious reading-room the world possesses, and explained the wonderful mechanical organization that brings almost every volume in that immense collection within a minute of one's hand. "With all this," I asked him, "why doesn't the place think?" He seemed, discreetly, to consider it did (**22** p. 237–238).

Just one month after the Nazi invasion of Poland in September 1939, Archibald MacLeish succeeded Herbert Putnam as Librarian of Congress. The nomination of MacLeish, a poet and man of letters, ignited a firestorm of criticism from the American Library Association, which believed the post should be held by a certified librarian. His friends, more gently, wondered aloud why he would interrupt his pursuit of the muse to take on a government position. In explaining why he accepted President Franklin Delano Roosevelt's appointment, MacLeish articulated a new and urgent mission not only for the Library of Congress but for all American libraries and librarians.

> Those of us who are concerned . . . with the preservation of the civilization and the inherited culture of this nation find ourselves in a situation in which time is running out, not like sand in a glass, but like the blood in an opened artery. . . .
>
> We will either educate the people of this Republic to know and therefore to value and therefore to preserve their own democratic culture or we will watch the people of this Republic trade their democratic culture for the nonculture, the obscurantism, the superstition, the brutality, the tyranny which is overrunning eastern and central and southern Europe (**15** p. 209).

MacLeish argued that, in this perilous era, librarians were not, as they should be, "opening that knowledge and that understanding to the citizens of the Republic." In his view, librarians everywhere should move from their passive role as collectors and preservers of the culture, to the affirmative obligation to proclaim the culture and make it understood.

The changes MacLeish made in the Library's administrative structure reflected his activist stance. In this work of reorganization, however, he acknowledged his debt to his predecessors, building on the outstanding efforts of Spofford in accumulating the Library's collections and on the work of Putnam in processing and organizing them.

REORGANIZATION OF THE LIBRARY

Before MacLeish's appointment, the Library was, he wrote, "not so much an organization in its own right as the lengthened shadow of a man—a man of great force, extraordinary abilities. . . . Only a man of Herbert Putnam's remarkable qualities could have administered an institution the size of the Library of Congress by direct and personal supervision of all its operations" (**14** p. 279). MacLeish's elegant prose continued:

> The principal difficulty with the old Library . . . was the fact that the whole fabric depended from the Librarian as the miraculous architecture of the paper wasp hangs from a single anchor. There was the Librarian—myself—in his vaulted office with his messenger outside. There was the chief assistant librarian . . . in a room across the hall, his desk piled with order slips and vouchers. There was the office of the secretary of the Library—for neither the Librarian nor the chief assistant librarian had a full-time secretary of his own. And below these two, dependent on them for immediate supervision and direction, were 35 different and separate administrative units (**14** p. 279).

With a burgeoning staff of twelve hundred employees and the compelling need to streamline the Library's operations as the shadow of war loomed larger, MacLeish decentralized control and delegated authority. General Order 964 for June 29, 1940, directed the establishment

ARCHIBALD MACLEISH AND LUTHER EVANS *(LEFT)* EXAMINE A BOOK
IN THE HISPANIC DIVISION, CA. 1940. LC-USP6-852-C

of the Reference Department, named Dr. Luther Evans and Mr. David Mearns director and assistant director respectively, and enumerated its functions—reference assistance, book selection, book service, and custodial duties.

The general order assigned twenty-five divisions to the department. The Main Reading Room was designated part of the Reading Rooms Division, together with the annex reading rooms, the study room service, the social sciences reference room, the local history and genealogy room, the reading room for the blind, and a proposed science and technology reading room.

Just as the war in Europe was a driving force in the Librarian's plans for service in the reading rooms, so also was it the chief obstacle in fulfilling those schemes. In fact, the Reference Department of the 1940 reorganization was a paper giant, a department in name only.

With the bombing of Pearl Harbor, the European war became the American war. As Library employees joined up, reading room manpower went down, while demands for service increased. MacLeish himself was tapped for services to President Roosevelt for more than a year. All these elements combined to delay the effective reorganization of the Reference Department until 1944.

One portion of reorganization that did not have to wait was MacLeish's definition of the Library's priorities of action. His famous Canons of Service specified the following:

1. The Library of Congress undertakes for Members of the Congress any and all research and reference projects bearing upon the Library's collections and required by Members in connection with the performance of their legislative duties.

2. The Library of Congress undertakes for officers and departments of government research projects, appropriate to the Library, which can be executed by reference to its collections, and which the staffs of offices and departments are unable to execute.

3. The reference staff and facilities of the Library of Congress are available to members of the public, universities, learned societies and other libraries requiring service which the Library staff is equipped to give and which can be given without interference with services to the Congress and other agencies of the Federal Government (**14** p. 303).

It is the third canon which most closely describes the policy guiding the work of the Main Reading Room down to the present day. Here is MacLeish's *explication de texte*:

This policy is active as well as passive. Passively considered it means that reference inquiries, and requests for bibliothecal service, which cannot be satisfied by other libraries or scholarly institutions nearer the inquirer, may be submitted to the Library of Congress which will respond to them within necessary limitations of time and labor. Actively considered, the Library's policy in this regard means that the Library of Congress, as the reference library of the people, holds itself charged with a duty to provide information to the people with regard to the materials they possess in its collections, and with an obligation to make its technical and scholarly services as broadly useful to the people as it can (**14** p. 303).

His phrase "the reference library of the people" asserted his matter-of-fact assumption that the people own the Library's collections. In the same fashion he emphasized the Library's educative and utilitarian mission to make its services widely available.

THE LIBRARY AT WAR

While reorganization waited, chilling evidence that the Library was on a war footing was everywhere. Author John Dos Passos, on a Guggenheim grant, worked in the Main Reading Room on biographical studies of several "founders of democratic habit in America." Using the Main Reading Room to conduct his research, I. F. Stone published *Business as Usual: The First Year of Defense* in 1941.

The year 1941 also saw the reading room staff surveying portions of the general collections to select books and pamphlets for preservation in the event of an emergency. In an intensive two-month period, reference assistants, aided by volunteers from other divisions, examined, book by book, over two million volumes and removed, labeled, and reshelved some 170,000 pieces "without interruption in our service," Superintendent Robert C. Gooch noted proudly. Reading room staff gave expanded and expedited services to the defense agencies and arranged for assignments of personnel to assist in certain defense library operations.

On September 10, a "democracy alcove" was established in the Main Reading Room for the use of visitors and readers.

> From the wealth of writings on democracy were assembled works on the Declaration of Independence and the Constitution, collections of and selections from the writings of American statesmen from the period of *The Federalist* to the present century, analyses of the theory and practice of democracy by American and foreign authors, primers prepared for students in our elementary schools, pamphlets from the time of Thomas Paine's *Common Sense* to the present crisis, poetry, drama, biography, and historical fiction. Copies of the mimeographed list of the material in the democracy collection have been distributed. . . . The influence of the idea was soon to be seen in its adoption by libraries elsewhere. . . . Commenting on the democracy alcove (based on our list) established at the Olean (N.Y.) public library, an editorial in a local newspaper said: "We have a long way to go before we will reach a condition of national understanding as to just what a democracy must be and what it will demand in the world of tomorrow. A 'democracy alcove' in every one of our public libraries should help our journey to a very considerable degree" (11 1941, p. 55–56).

Personnel vacancies and turnovers also created problems. Because of the deficiencies of a shorthanded and undertrained staff, regular service invariably suffered. One casualty was advice to readers on using the Public Catalog. The 1941 annual report noted that "the pressure of work at the central desk in the Main Reading Room is such that assistants are frequently unable to assist readers in this regard." Speaking of the demands on reading room staff, the report continued, "The pressure for speed is great, as are the demands for locating and delivering large quantities of material and the ready furnishing of information in response to reference inquiries" (11 1941, p. 192–193):

Low salaries, as well as stressful working conditions contributed to turnover.

> The compensation for work in the entering positions, $1,200 and $1,260 per year, is now so much below wages which can be commanded elsewhere in the government that it is becoming increasingly difficult to hold employees until they can be trained and promoted. It must also be pointed out that the duties of these positions are onerous and the conditions of work, particularly in the stacks of the main building, very trying. The only measures which would provide a real solution for this problem are an increase in the entering salaries and rotation of employees in the less desirable types of work (11 1941, p. 193).

That Mr. MacLeish was aware of these problems is evident. In his appropriations request for fiscal 1941, he emphasized that his first priority was to improve the salary situation. In April the Civil Service Commission agreed, at his request, "to conduct a survey of the Library in order to adjust existing inequalities of classification, to correct the allocation of positions where duties had undergone a gradual change over a period of years, and to bring the classification of all positions into line with that of the government service generally" (11 1941, p. 332).

As the war continued, later annual reports noted that the reading room staff and "the strength of the collections" have been repeatedly tested by the needs of the government war agencies. In addition, continuing demands on the reading room staff to assist in the selection and evacuation of materials for safekeeping resulted, in 1942, in a curtailment of service to the public. The Main Reading Room closed at 6:00 P.M. rather than 10:00 P.M., but maintained a small staff to care for the collections and to answer telephone inquiries. Late in 1942, stack access, which had been restricted in 1941, was discontinued totally. There were over 350 staff changes in 1942, including 71 resignations and 29 military furloughs.

In 1944, a significant step for reference assistants was taken. Their duty station was moved from the center desk to the alcoves just beyond the card catalog. In that traditional location staff had become largely "preoccupied with the dispatching of book requisitions and the removal of volumes from the conveyors. . . . The move resulted in a marked increase in the proportion of readers receiving personal attention. Advice on the use of the Catalog can now be given, searches for books or information can be extended over wider areas, problems can be thoroughly studied" (**11** 1944, p. 89).

Some of these problems were presented by men from the armed forces who are "increasingly using the general reading rooms for studies collateral with their technical and administrative courses. . . . The reference staff has assisted them in the preparation of manuals on such subjects as trucking pools and the techniques of amphibious operations. Other enlisted personnel have taken advantage of their presence in Washington and the accessibility of the Library of Congress to pursue their academic interests" (**11** 1944, p. 89).

For the Justice Department, reference staff found biographical information on "subversive persons" and, for the War Department, information on the next of kin of soldiers killed or missing in action. This necessary concentration on war work affected service to other readers.

On March 25, 1944, the reorganization of the Reference Department became official. General Order 1218 created the General Reference and Bibliography Division, which included the following reading rooms—Main, Thomas Jefferson, Local History and Genealogy, and Slavic. The division was located within the Public Reference Service.

MacLeish did not stay to watch the effects of his new policies. Even during his tenure as Librarian, he had been drawn by President Roosevelt into the international arena; in December the president nominated him to the post of assistant secretary of state in charge of public and cultural affairs. On December 19, MacLeish resigned as Librarian to go to the State Department, leaving the Library in the hands of Luther Harris Evans as Acting Librarian. It was Evans, the successor, who described the effects of MacLeish's five-year tenure as "the brush of the comet." MacLeish's sweeping reorganizations and enunciation of the Canons of Service touched the library like a force of nature, and left it changed forever.

A comet is a very hard act to follow. But Luther Harris Evans, who after all had applied that term to his predecessor, knew exactly how to set about it. In a radio address delivered over station WTOP on July 21, 1945, Librarian Evans disclaimed any need for "revolutionary change by a new Librarian of Congress."

There is, however, one important difference between the years just past and those just ahead, and I foresee that there will of necessity be considerable change, though it be made gradually and cautiously. The years of the MacLeish administration were years of war, war for the world and, for most of the period, war for the United States. The approaching years will be years of peace, and they will bring new obligations and new means of service. . . . The war has shown as never before the importance of the task to which all librarians are dedicated; it has demonstrated beyond question that knowledge, precise knowledge, must form the basis of all Government policies and private programs, that knowledge has become so extensive and complicated in our modern world there can be no hope of controlling it except in terms of great research libraries giving a highly responsive service at all points where programs are developed and policies decided. . . .

It is from a conviction that the national library, and beyond it the great system of university, research, and public libraries, are sources of essential light without which the national life would be darkened, and the further conviction that good library management can perform statesmanlike services for the people of this Nation, that I draw inspiration for my service as the Librarian of Congress (**11** 1945, p. 21).

Named Acting Librarian from December 19, 1944, through June 29, 1945, Dr. Evans was nominated as Librarian of Congress by President Truman on June 18 and assumed the office on June 30, 1945. From his work as director of the Legislative Reference Service and as Chief Assistant Librarian, he knew the Library well. And, as is evident from the speech above, which was given only a month after his permanent appointment, Evans had an agenda and a vision for the Library.

Just as he realized that knowledge and its control was the key to a peaceful world, so he understood that the acquisition and arrangement of that knowledge were not the only tasks of a great library.

If the Library of Congress is to be a hand to lead to knowledge, rather than frantic fingers to clutch at it, there must be a human development concurrent with the development of material—more sorters and searchers and accessioners, more catalogers and classifiers and shelflisters, more bibliographers and subject specialists and regionalists. Until Dr. Bush's "memex" or other "cheap complex devices of great reliability" come on the market, we must look to persons for the governance of these vast accumulations. So far, the genius of invention has been more completely successful in proliferating records than in creating automata for identifying, digesting and interpreting them. It is this circumstance, this elusive equation which impels the enlistment of the most talented and resourceful minds.

But there is now a need not only for more builders of bibliographical apparatus but for expositors also who will translate it into action and result. For this, specialists of great competence must be found, men and women, willing, by themselves forsaking, to find, paradoxically, a greater distinction than in the classroom and in the laboratory and in personal research (**11** 1945, p. 17–18).

Staff members met this challenge, being consistently commended for their competence. Many of the "expositors" and "specialists of great competence" mentioned by Evans were to be found in the Main Reading Room. Job descriptions for these positions indicate that the assistants in charge needed at a minimum a college degree and graduation from an accredited library school or equivalent training and experience. Also desirable was experience (three years or more) in reference and bibliography in a large research library. The senior reference assistants needed a college degree and a master's in their subject field, as well as an MLS or equivalent training and experience.

THE READING ROOM RETURNS TO A PEACETIME FOOTING

The General Reference and Bibliography Division report (10A 1945, p. 10) for the first year of the peace shows the Main Reading Room staff heavily engaged in assisting government and private researchers to return to peacetime activities. Chief Robert C. Gooch remarked that the reader constituency—researchers from federal offices and local educational institutions—remained fairly constant, with a notable exception:

> Late in the year a noticeable increase was observed in the number of service men seeking information on veterans' rights and benefits and advice on post war education and the problems of small business. Of particular interest have been the many instances in which men of the armed forces on furlough, or on temporary assignment in the area, have visited the Library to renew for even a brief period studies interrupted by the war.

It was expected that the trend among readers would be to academic studies, a development Gooch "anticipated by the contraction of the war area." But grim reminders of the war were evident in the list of services rendered in the Main Reading Room to government and active military personnel. These included reference assistance on such topics as disposal of surplus war property, treaties, war contracts, and crucial experiments in physiology which required the use of animals. Also mentioned were translations of autopsy reports from German, documentary sources on German atrocities in the war, plans for the liquidation of certain agencies with the resultant transfer of records, and, for the Naval Medical Research Institute, the creation of a term to describe the fitting of artificial fingers to mutilated hands. "Digito-palmar prosthesis" was suggested and accepted.

Staff also spent time on reference collection development. In the weeks following D-Day, they organized a special collection of five hundred books on postwar planning for placement in Alcove 6. Echoing the establishment in 1941 of the "democracy alcove," it was another signal that the era of peace was beginning and proved a popular and useful supplement to the reference collection.

By the end of 1946, the "personal attention provided" by the reading room reference assistants was severely limited. An appendix to the Librarian's annual report for that year includes the Library's budget justification for fiscal year 1947 and provides a very detailed picture of the General Reference and Bibliography Division.

> The present staff . . . numbers 56 assistants, 9 of whom are assigned to the compilation of bibliographies and to work on reference correspondence and 16 to reference work in the general reading rooms. The personnel is not adequate to give a reference and bibliographical service commensurate in extent and quality with the size of the Library's collection or with the importance of the demands made upon it, nor to supervise the reference work performed in the annex. More important, the staff cannot answer all the reference requests received and the number of

such requests has increased notably this year as has the number of readers served in the general reading room.

At present the staff is able to devote only 5 minutes to each reader although an average of 10 to 15 minutes is necessary for adequate service. Because of the work-load, the function of compiling bibliographies and lists has had to be slighted to the disadvantage of the Government agencies requesting them. If the Library is to fulfill its obligation to the Government not only to maintain its collections but to assist investigators in finding needed information locked within the pages of its volumes, it must increase its reference staff and establish additional bibliographic controls, both of which proved critically deficient during the war and are unequal to the task of assisting with the problems confronting the Government and American industry in this new era.

The peacetime reduction of government operational hours had an immediate impact on service in the reading room. Chief Robert Gooch in his division report for 1946 commented, "Conversion of the Government workweek from six to five days immediately brought larger numbers of serious readers into the reading rooms on Saturdays. With no retraction in services to readers or inquiries by telephone, the regular hours of opening in the reading rooms were continued throughout the entire year at additional overtime compensation for week-end work" (p. 4).

Although the additional positions requested for 1947 would, if granted, have alleviated some staffing shortages, Mr. Gooch was also unhappy about the current grade allocations:

> The Public Reference Section has suffered neglect, except in a minor number of positions, partly because of the preponderance of war service appointees and promotees and constantly changing personnel, and partly because of the relatively unfavorable conception of reference work by the Civil Service Commission. Betterment of grades in this Section will require, apparently, a new view and interpretation of the service, to the end that general reference work in a vast collection such as the Library's will receive recognition comparable to that accorded special reference work in sharply defined fields and much smaller collections (p. 25).

The 1947 annual report of the division presented a brighter picture. Three staff members returned safely from active military service. The long-sought classification survey got under way, and the chief recommended that the positions in the Public Reference Section be given priority.

Staff discontent was noted in several other areas, however, and a number of discussions ensued. Improvements included the installation of more powerful lights in the Main Reading Room alcoves and accelerated work on the Annex catalog. Discussions of efficiency ratings and what they meant continued until the chief acknowledged that "the Public Reference Section has been generally noted for its *esprit de corps*, notwithstanding occasional rough stones in its structure, and the effort and stress involved in performing even 'adequate' work under very taxing circumstances quite naturally leads to the expectation that the effort and stress will be the primary consideration in the efficiency ratings. There is still no comfort or satisfaction in being 'good'" (**10A** 1947, p. 52). The level of stress and effort may be guessed at by considering that the reading rooms provided reference service to 267,250 readers in 1947, "a very considerable increase" over the total of 117,725 the previous year.

The Librarian's annual report noted two trends in reader interests: "Lessening concern on the part of official agencies with postwar planning and an increasing attention to international affairs and relations; and, on the part of the non-official public, an increased interest in self-improvement, together with the greater maturity of the student clientele at the university level, reflecting the experience and objectivity of the veterans who have swelled the university rolls" (**11** 1947, p. 32).

For the remainder of Evans's tenure, he paid more and more attention to international affairs and relations. At the Library he emphasized blanket order arrangements for purchasing current foreign materials and agreements for the international exchange of official publications. Outside the Library, he became increasingly involved in UNESCO. He served the international organization in various capacities while Librarian and also directed the Library's participation in many aspects of UNESCO's activities. The Library and UNESCO addressed problems of standardization of bibliographical controls and the development of the Universal Copyright Convention (**18** p. 235).

Evans's increasing emphasis on international affairs roused some ire in the Congress. This congressional displeasure became explicit in the budget hearings of 1952, but may also have contributed to the budget cuts suffered by the Library in 1948. For the General Reference and Bibliography Division, these cuts resulted in the loss of seven positions; the reading room lost 20 percent of its staff. The budget cut also forced a curtailment in evening service on Mondays and Fridays, resulting in a 10 percent cut in service. Even with these losses of hours and librarians, the staff answered 2,287 more telephone inquiries, 6,667 more readers' questions, and 1,325 more reference letters than in 1947. Staff morale, buffeted by the curtailments, was raised considerably by the successful conclusion of the classification review, which recommended advancements for many of the reference positions.

Although in 1946 the chief was unhappy that staff shortages forced the limitation of service to five minutes per reader, a study done in 1947 gave this figure some legitimacy. The Librarian's annual report summarized an attempt to estimate the average time required per reader to give satisfactory service.

> It was discovered that a very large number of questions can be answered in 5 minutes, but that others require up to 15 or 30 minutes, or even more. During the year 5,481 instances were noted in the last group. While studies of this question are proceeding, it appears at present that not less than 10 minutes is a fair average allowance per reader for reference service, and that the true figure is probably closer to 15 minutes.

The Stack and Reader Division, responsible for the custody and service of the general classified collections and their service especially in the Main Reading Room, in the Thomas Jefferson Room, and in the study rooms, also undertook an operational study. The Librarian's report commented:

> Here, in spite of the shorter hours of opening, more books were delivered than in the previous year, the total being 1,630,839 books to 586,226 readers. A survey conducted by this Division of the time consumed in bringing books from the shelves to the readers' desks, shows that the average time in the Main Reading Room (from the filing of the request to the delivery of the book) was 16 minutes for books in the Main Building, and 23 minutes for books in the Annex (p. 42).

In 1951, in an attempt to streamline reading room service, the telephone service was shifted from Alcove 6 to an area nearer the front door. "The purpose of this change would be to provide some preliminary guidance to the public or readers as they enter the reading room, to answer immediately certain types of questions, and to enable readers requiring additional service to be referred by the telephone assistant or her assistant on duty to the most appropriate reference assistant" (**10A** 1952, p. 8).

By 1952 the high subject competence of the reference assistants was such that they had difficulty making themselves available to reading room patrons. They had acquired considerable experience with the diverse collections and resources of the Library. "By virtue thereof, they have to be on call more and more to serve the needs of the Library itself. With increasing frequency, we have had to call upon the general reference assistants . . . to provide specialized service . . . and special reference assignments on the request of the Library's administrative family. . . . The staff, already pared down to a minimum because of budgetary requirements, is increasingly used in service beyond that indicated by the term, Public Reference Service" (**10A** 1952, p. 3).

The effects of age and steady use were seen in many parts of the building and the reading room. The annual report observed that:

> The conveyors, which carried books from shelves to those who wanted them were old and, what was worse, were worn. For more than fifty years they had made their endless rounds. They were not silent now. Now they clanged as they moved by, making grumbling protest against postponement of their replacement. Occasionally a cable would snap, or they would crumple on themselves, and they would halt until hurried, emergency repairs would release them to their mission.
>
> When such accidents occurred, there would be delays and delay would sap patience and there would be inconvenience. It was not unusual for an important book, importantly expected, to be destroyed when the conveyors jammed, and brass fingers sliced them into futile strips of paper. These unhappy episodes were few, but they were increasing. By and large, however, the service was good, and the muscles of the staff were able to compensate for mechanical failures. And the figure of Time, bearded and transfixed, before "Mr. Flanagan's Clock" in the reading room was still a statuesque expression of belief that time stood still in the Library (**11** 1949, p. 56).

It did not, of course, and Burton W. Adkinson, director of the Reference Department in whose care the Main Reading Room fell, was conscious of time's toll. In his 1950 report, he wrote:

> Much of the equipment . . . was designed for the opening of the Main Building and has become worn or obsolete. . . . It is hoped that funds will be available in the next fiscal year to provide for the centralization of the carrier and tube systems in the Main Reading Room. This single change will not only effect greater efficiency but will make possible the saving of one position and the substitution of a lower grade position for another. A program of reader chair replacement has also been prepared for this reading room. Many of the original chairs have been worn out through fifty years of use and substitute chairs of a different design have been used to replace them (p. 14).

While this history of the Main Reading Room is filled with statistics on books delivered, readers served, questions answered, and the staff who answered them, the story cannot be told without some mention of the readers themselves, for it is their presence and their need that gives the Library purpose. To remedy this lack of attention, and because every word in the following account is as true today as when it was written, Dr. Evans's graceful tribute to our readership is presented here:

> These readers, it should be understood, have come unannounced, unsponsored and unexplained. They have not been obliged in any way to qualify themselves. The doors have swung inward, and their entrance has been recorded by no more formality than a clicking sound on an auto-

matic counter. They have gone straight to the catalog. . . . When difficulties have been encountered, there have been attendants eager to help. They have sent for their books, the books have been delivered to the desk of their choosing, and, when they have finished with them, they have departed. This Library has been, like most American libraries, absolutely free; it has been dedicated to its users.

But who were these readers? Nobody knew. Most of them were citizens of these States, but there were thousands whose accent and demeanor suggested foreign origin. Some, it seemed likely, were described in the pages of a Who's Who. Some, though by no means the majority, were yet to attain distinction. It was possible that at any hour of the day a brilliant faculty for a great university could be recruited from the men and women in that octagon, unaware of one another, but brought together by a common quest of learning. There were other types of course, and they represented other conditions of life and other objects. It was sometimes disturbing to the *amour propre* to observe how often a love of books attracted those who might have found asylum somewhere else. Yet it was clear that all of them attributed their presence to a serious purpose.

What could be said of the reader in those reading rooms was that he or she was at least sixteen years old, frequently literate, and ordinarily mindful of an errand. . . . There were some who came and went with the gay lope of halfbacks entering or leaving a game, others whose spirits overcame reluctance in their legs, still others who were wheeled about in the noiseless chairs of invalids. There were repeaters, those who came day after day, who were there at opening and remained until the blinking lights dispersed them. And there were those who appeared for a week or so and vanished into differing pursuits (**11** 1949, p. 55–56).

Readers, too, suffered the effects of budget cuts such as reductions in hours of service. But they survived and continued to come, adapting to changed schedules of service, but not without inconvenience as "the very weight of the number of readers on Saturday afternoons caused an overflow from the Main Reading Room to the Government Publications Reading Room, causing them to stand and wait for a seat or desk to be vacated" (**10A** 1950, p. 5).

THE END OF AN ERA

A somber note sounded in 1952. The Library had been steadily losing ground in the appropriations process, and now the congressional displeasure with Dr. Evans came into the open. While Evans was attending a UNESCO executive board meeting in Paris, budget hearings were held in March before the House Appropriations Committee. Two of its members, Christopher McGrath of New York and Walt Horan of Washington, suggested that Evans "get another job someplace." Horan bluntly stated, "He is not running the Library. Perhaps he should be associated with the State Department." Although Verner Clapp, who was representing the Library at the hearings, strongly defended Evans as a man who worked eighteen hours a day and weekends and kept in constant touch with the Library during his absences, some congressmen were never completely convinced that Evans was effectively fulfilling his responsibilities on Capitol Hill (**18** p. 235).

On July 1, 1953, Dr. Evans was elected as the third director-general of UNESCO and resigned the office of Librarian effective July 5. Although his stewardship of the Library was not always popular with the Congress, his achievements were impressive. Taking the helm in the last months of the war, he led the Library into the new era of peace. Because he recognized the importance of global information in a world changed forever by war, he turned the Library's attention and grasp outward. For Evans, the "obligations of peace" included the obligation to work toward the attainment of international harmony. His years at the Library, no less than his tenure at UNESCO, testify to his success.

After the meteoric MacLeish and the internationalist Evans, Congress, perceiving a lack of attention to congressional needs, grew restive. It made known its displeasure in the May 19, 1954, hearings before the House Committee on Appropriations. "The new Librarian should be mindful that the Library is the instrument and the creature of Congress. Its duties historically have been to meet the needs of the Members of Congress first and to limit its service to others to that which can be furnished with the funds and staff available" (**8** p. 50).

L. Quincy Mumford, nominated by President Eisenhower to the post of Librarian of Congress on April 19, heard the complaint clearly during the July 26, 1954, hearings before the Senate Rules and Administration Committee. One senator asked him plaintively: ". . . if you found that the Library of Congress was neglecting its primary duty—that for which it was established—that of service to the Congress, would you be willing to correct that situation?" (nomination hearings, 83d Congress, July 26, 1954, p. 9).

Mumford acknowledged that his first task would be to restore congressional confidence in the Library's willingness to adhere to the 1940 Canons of Service mandating assistance to Congress as the Library's first responsibility. He was confirmed by the Senate, without objection, on July 29 and took office on September 1, 1954.

THE FIRST MUMFORD DECADE: ACTIVITY IN THE MAIN READING ROOM

Mr. Mumford's adherence to the Canons of Service and his promises to the Congress affected the work of the Main Reading Room. In the 1956 report of the General Reference and Bibliography Division, chief Henry J. Dubester reiterated the division's reference standards and recognized its duty to the Congress:

> With the exception of the reorganization of 1944, which joined the bibliography division to the reading room service, the essential functions of the division trace back at least to the time that this Library first began to render service in its own building. Senior members of the staff, still in active service, were trained by predecessors who took part in that move. This staff has been influential in developing a climate within which the service of the division is rendered. It is a climate which thinks first of all of the relationship of the Library to the Congress which it is designed to serve. It is a climate in which experience has demonstrated that the small errors of today become the source of major complaints of the morrow. It reflects a spirit which dictates that no request can be slighted, or be given summary treatment, lest the ripple of enlarged consequences eventually do major hurt to significant (or what is thought significant) activities (p. 1).

This experienced staff numbered seventeen men and women who provided reference assistance in the alcoves of the Main Reading Room, at the telephone inquiry desk near the entrance to the room, and in the Thomas Jefferson Room in the Annex. Although the provision of reference service in the two major public reading rooms was their main duty, these librarians performed library functions across the board. Acquisitions, bibliography, and special projects were a few of the tasks they carried out. Dubester strongly asserted this point in the 1958 report: "A large staff, compared to the staffs of other large research libraries, it is

"THE GREAT DOMED ROTUNDA READING ROOM . . . IS MARKED BY A MAGNIFICENCE OF
ARCHITECTURE AND DECORATION NOWHERE ELSE TO BE FOUND IN THE BUILDING. . . .
SCULPTURE AND PAINTINGS, RARE MARBLES, AND A BROAD SCHEME OF COLOR AND OF
ORNAMENTATION IN STUCCO RELIEF UNITE WITH A LOFTY ARCHITECTURAL DESIGN TO
FORM WHAT IS ONE OF THE MOST NOTABLE INTERIORS IN THE COUNTRY"
(HERBERT SMALL, *THE LIBRARY OF CONGRESS: ITS ARCHITECTURE AND DECORATION*).

nevertheless under constant pressure to perform its primary duties of public reference work as well as the host of additional tasks assigned to it which run the gamut of library functions" (**IOA** 1958, p. 1).

Librarians selected materials for the Main Reading Room reference collection and also had responsibility, because of their specialized subject competence, for recommending acquisitions in the following fields: religion, philosophy, psychology, local history, genealogy, military art and science, foreign language and specialized dictionaries, English and American history, French literature and history, economics, sociology, and reference works in general.

The Public Reference Section in this decade continued to field a wide range of questions— questions which were often topical. In 1959 "reference questions were concentrated on American history and government, especially on the statehood of Alaska and Hawaii, the Lincoln Sesquicentennial, the construction of the new East Front of the Capitol. The Lebanon crisis brought the most inquiries in the foreign field" (**IOA** 1959, p. 7).

A *Sports Illustrated* story, in that year, earned the staff a bit of publicity. The editor sought identification for "To sin by silence." Neither he nor "a number of librarians and scholars in New York" could determine who had coined the phrase. The reading room staff quickly confirmed Ella Wheeler Wilcox as the author. The magazine applauded the Public Reference Section in the October 20 issue.

A review of the questions asked in 1960–61 by the public, the press, and government agencies indicates great concern over national and international affairs, such as the presidential election and events in Cuba, Asia, and Africa. Questions on inaugural ceremonies became so numerous in the weeks before the inauguration of John F. Kennedy that a special reference collection was temporarily assembled. The Freedom March on Washington in August 1963 also stimulated many reference inquiries.

Despite the volume, the Main Reading Room librarians answered the many questions thoroughly and efficiently, remembering that the public expected "superior and 'last word' service" from the Library of Congress. With good conscience they could have readily accepted the awkward but undoubtedly sincere praise of one reader: "You do dredge up pearls and nuggets from the ooze of your copious files" (**IOA** 1957, p. 13).

Over the decade Main Reading Room librarians also demonstrated their expertise in a variety of areas and projects: they compiled a card bibliography of Irish contributions to the development of the United States; for UNESCO, a list of centennials of births and deaths of prominent Americans; and a list of source materials on gardens for the blind. They completed a survey of special collections on magic and the supernatural for possible acquisition by the Library.

For the Librarian's use in planning for a third building, the staff provided a bibliography of current materials on library buildings and equipment. They also worked on a series of literary centenaries ranging from the 350th anniversary of the King James Bible to the centennial of Longfellow's "Paul Revere's Ride." Henry Dubester was complimentary of the Main Reading Room staff, writing:

> With respect to the problems of professional staffing, we feel that we have developed a rather balanced staff as regards experience and length of service versus infusion of new blood and new outlooks, and with respect to subject coverage provided by the experience and academic backgrounds of the individual staff members. It is recognized, however, that added strength is very necessary at the subprofessional level to round out what is now potentially an unexcelled group of reference librarians (**IOA** 1957, p. 3).

Milton Lomask, author of *Odd Destiny: A Life of Alexander Hamilton*, dedicated his book to one of the Main Reading Room librarians. The inscription—"One of the nobler beings, second only to guardian angels and honest mechanics, is a good reference librarian"—could have been the encomium for the work of all the Main Reading Room librarians during the first decade of the Mumford years.

In spite of the staff's acknowledged subject competence and involvement with special projects, the salaries—or grade levels, which ranged from GS-7 to GS-12—left much to be desired. Dubester explained:

> We have faced the problem of recruiting staff at the GS-7 level, requiring academic library training and desiring specialized subject competence as well. Although we have been inordinately successful . . . we nevertheless have been compelled to recognize that the newer additions to our staff still lack much in comparison to many senior members who have remained at the GS-7 level for many years. The classification problems involved have so far stopped any progress toward rectification of grade allocations. We hope to secure recognition of the GS-7 level as the entering trainee stage, and the GS-9 grade as the journeyman reference librarian. Such recognition will influence the grade disposition throughout the division, if not throughout the Library, and will require serious review. Nevertheless, the present relationship does harbor serious inequities which must, in all fairness to the individuals concerned, be resolved in their favor (**IOA** 1957, p. 24).

Another perennial problem, solved over the years with varying degrees of success, is that of staff scheduling. An early mention of the dilemma described a review undertaken in 1956 of all activities in the Public Reference Section in hopes of finding a way to schedule staff to give them uninterrupted time for special research and reference correspondence. But the report concluded: "The result has been very disappointing. At best, the schedule permits one halfday per week for each member of the staff to be freed for such assignment, and this does not appear very practical" (**IOA** 1956, p. 11).

The work environment too left much to be desired; in his annual report for 1954 Dubester explained apologetically that

> We have deferred recommending purchase of better equipment for the professional reference staff in the reference alcoves in the Main Reading Room. Their quarters are crowded and their facilities are limited and do not contribute to maximum efficiency. With the possibilities of major shifts in space arrangements due to the continued growth problem caused by the Main Catalog, current expenditure for new equipment may be wasteful, but should no major moves be forthcoming in the immediate future we shall look forward to the purchase of small desks with adequate drawer space for each of the reference assistants on duty in the Main Reading Room (p. 8).

His fears about wasteful expenditures were groundless. Once purchased, those desks were in use until December 1987 when the Main Reading Room closed for its second renovation.

Tension between the Reference Information and Telephone Inquiry Unit and the librarians in the alcoves was another minor irritant. The Reference Information and Telephone Inquiry Unit, located near the entrance to the reading room, shared in the room's service by giving guidance to entering readers and by answering telephone requests (10,717 individuals and 24,416 calls were handled in 1956). With only two regular positions the unit relied on the alcove librarians for support. Librarians in the alcoves resented serving in the Reference Information and Telephone Inquiry Unit. They decried the disruption in their workday, the reduction in effectiveness of alcove reference activity, and their inability to complete the multitude of secondary tasks that a strong reference program requires, successful service to its public notwithstanding.

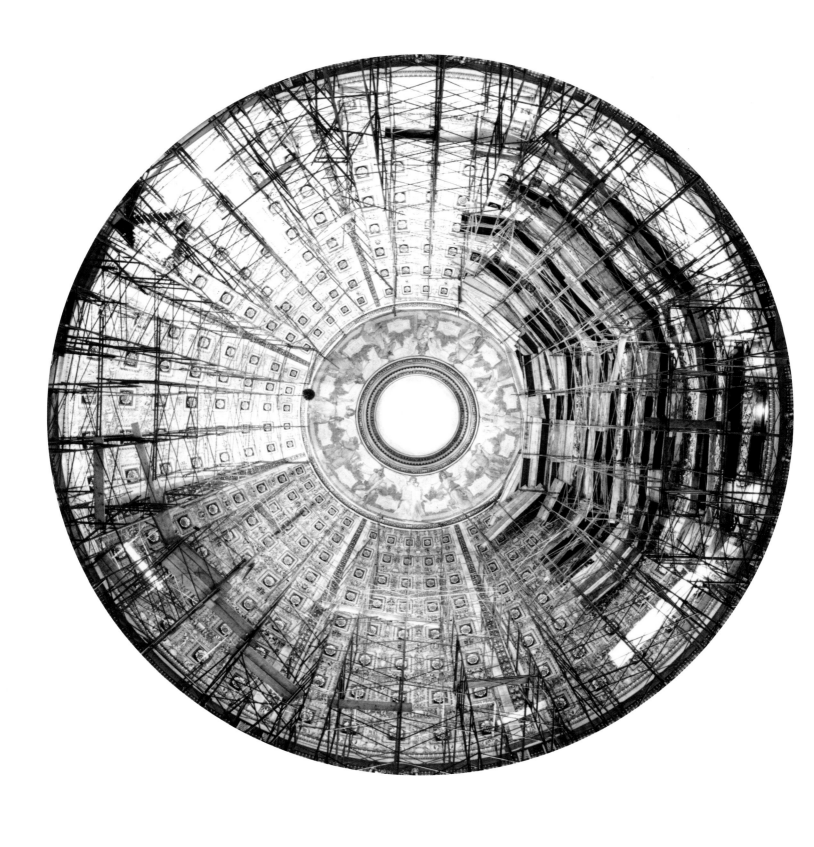

THE INTRICATE SCAFFOLDING FOR THE DOME CLEANING AND RESTORATION,
JANUARY 1965. (PHOTOGRAPH BY AINSWORTH JOHNSON.) LC-USP6-4558-C

Administrators of the Main Reading Room continued to grapple with the less important but annoyingly perennial problem of what to do with high school students. Dubester wrote: "We have found that the younger readers require more in the way of assistance and lean heavily upon the advice of our reference service. . . . Such service to immature students . . . deprives the more serious reader and scholar from the benefits of our reference service" (**10** 1954, p. 5–6).

His hand-wringing prose calls to mind the 1944 exclusion from the Main Reading Room of "roving adolescents" bent on "social intercourse." It was not until 1958, however, that Mr. Mumford, with the concurrence of the Joint Committee on the Library, issued General Order 1664 on the use of the Library of Congress by high school students. Beginning on September 1, 1958, only high school students who presented a letter from their principal or headmaster certifying the student's specific need to use the Library's research resources were to be admitted.

THE FIRST RENOVATION

The first ten years of the Mumford administration ended with the closing of the Main Reading Room—for the first time since it opened in 1897—on May 4, 1964, to permit renovation and the installation of air-conditioning. Robert H. Land, the new chief of General Reference and Bibliography, the parent body of the reading room, praised the staff for its part in preparing for the closing: "The entire Public Reference Section is to be commended for its calm assistance in the move and for interpreting it to readers, thereby securing their understanding rather than their criticism" (**10A** 1964, p. 3).

The closing of the room and the moving of staff and collections took place relatively smoothly:

> From March 31, when a start was made on the erection of over 300 units of temporary shelving for the alcoves collection of approximately 27,000 volumes, through May 1, books, furniture, and telephones were moved and the staff relocated, with most members in the Annex. The whole process was marked by the utmost cooperation and effectiveness of the various divisions and departments concerned . . . and what was feared to be difficult was actually accomplished with unbelievable ease (**10A** 1964, p. 3).

During the renovation period, readers used the Thomas Jefferson and North Reading Rooms in the Annex, and on Monday, August 16, 1965, "the room reopened for service. Five minutes later the first call slip was turned in at the great circular desk by Anne Harvey, a candidate for a master's degree in Spanish literature, and business had begun" (**11** 1965, p. 19).

THE SECOND MUMFORD DECADE: REFERENCE ACTIVITIES

The role played by the Main Reading Room librarians in the second decade is probably best illustrated by a passage in the division's 1972 annual report:

> Within the Library of Congress, the Main Reading Room—housing the main card catalog and a 25,000-volume reference collection—is the research hub. Reference service to patrons in the Main and the Thomas Jefferson Reading Rooms is provided by the Public Reference Section of the General Reference and Bibliography (GR&B) Division. Since they frequently refer readers to one or more of the Library's 15 specialized reading rooms, the public reference librarians need a broad knowledge of LC's collections and services. They must also be adept at answering questions on virtually every subject: in 1972, for example, sample inquiries concerned Great Britain's poet laureate, the stage history of Ibsen's *The Doll House*, the Florida delegates to the 1948 Pro-

gressive Party convention, adoption agencies, and the speeches of Henry Clay in the Kentucky legislature (**IOA** 1972, p. 9).

Staff members continued to function as well-rounded information agents, offering "quality-fashion" services. Reference queries were as usual varied, and interesting, and oftentimes mirrored foreign and domestic happenings. For example, in 1966, "events creating heavy reference demands were the deaths of Adlai E. Stevenson and Albert Schweitzer, Pope Paul's visit to the United Nations, the election in Great Britain, the election of Mrs. Indira Gandhi as Prime Minister of India and her visit to the United States, the visit of Princess Margaret, and the impending marriage of Miss Luci B. Johnson" (**IOA** 1966, p. 8).

Eight years later, in 1974, the reference inquiries continued to show great variety.

Many were topical: parliamentary trials, impeachment proceedings against President Nixon, resignations of Vice Presidents, the presidential administration with the most cabinet changes, financing of election campaigns, and the origin of "hush money." Among other subjects there were queries about the leading national producer of goat's milk, depreciation of telephone poles, women in the arts, and imports of seaweed (**IOA** 1974, p. 8).

ENTER TECHNOLOGY

Traditional reference practices continued to flourish in the Main Reading Room, but the librarians' reference horizons had begun to change. Librarians now recognized the compelling effect that automation could have on searching and retrieving material.

Some years earlier, "the very patrician Senator Saltonstall leaned across a hearings table" and said to Librarian of Congress Mumford, "I have had a continuing interest in the subject of mechanization of libraries . . . [and] it is a subject that we could ask [you] to work on and possibly present as a part of [your] request to the Bureau of the Budget next year. . . . As I understand it, it assists a person in getting information on a complicated subject or on any subject from a library. Just how, I am very frank to say, is completely over my head" (**7** p. 1).

Mumford answered:

We have had an internal committee since early in 1958 studying what is being done in business and in industry and in government elsewhere. . . . We are intensely interested in the matter and wish to progress as the means are available for doing this . . . [but] we realized that we must approach it cautiously, because the cost in equipment in this area is enormous, and we certainly do not wish to start junking our conventional methods of control of information. . . . We are at the present time contemplating trying to assign one person to devote himself exclusively to this thing (**7** p. 1).

"Mechanization" did not reach the Main Reading Room for some time, but there were intimations. The first signs appeared in the division report for 1962. The chief, Henry J. Dubester, wrote an article, "Libraries and Information Retrieval," which was published in the November 1962 issue of *American Behavioral Scientist*. In it he discussed computers and research libraries. That same year he read a paper "The Librarian and the Machine" at the University of Minnesota. Dubester, described in *American Behavioral Scientist* as "a leader of the current movement to rationalize the basic processes of scientific intelligence," was certainly giving thought to the possibilities of automation.

The reading room staff became actively involved in 1966. Their major task in the area of automation was the production of a computer-produced catalog of the Main Reading Room's reference collection. Work on the project began in 1967–68. A "most noteworthy develop-

THE NEWLY REFURBISHED MAIN READING ROOM, AUGUST 1965. LC-USP6-4783-C

ment was the launching in September of the project for a computer-produced catalog of the MRR Alcove collection. . . . Much was accomplished: thorough weeding of the collection of over 20,000 volumes in 20 classes was virtually completed with the assistance of the regular Public Reference staff. . . . Many problems were unraveled" and many conferences were held, "especially regarding the coding of computer tapes" (**10A** 1968, p. 6).

The Librarian's 1972 annual report revealed that

> There was tangible evidence of progress in the effort to develop a computer-produced book catalog for the Main Reading Room reference collection. Production began on a catalog of the monographs in the collection. It will be in three parts: subject; call number; and author, title, and added entry. By the end of the fiscal year the subject portion had been completed and was in use within the Library. Work continued on the preparation of entries for the serials in the collection (**11** 1972, p. 35).

The 1973 annual report not only praised the usefulness of the catalog, but acknowledged the success of the reading room's first major automated product. "Development of a computerized book catalog of the Main Reading Room's reference collection has for several years been a major undertaking of the Public Reference Section. . . . The catalog data base now contains approximately 11,500 monographic and 2,400 serial titles. This catalog and its future cumulations or supplements are expected to be a notable contribution to reference service everywhere; in the meantime, the several parts of the preliminary book catalog are proving to be useful within the Library" (**11** 1973, p. 52).

Modernization was going on elsewhere in the reading room. "To assist readers in finding their way through the many reference alcoves, over 200 signs were installed indicating subjects and heavily used titles, and diagrams were posted and distributed to readers." For a while in 1965 semimonthly meetings were held to acquaint new readers with the Library's reference services and facilities. Photocopiers were installed in the Main Reading Room in 1972. Readers were pleased that these labor-saving machines were available but were also frequently annoyed because they broke down so often.

The Mumford years spanned two decades of Library service devoted to Congress and the nation. Mumford, the first library-degree holder to attain the highest library position in the land, superintended a period of growth and progress. He saw the James Madison Memorial Building, the third building of the Library, out of planning and into construction before his retirement. He also supervised the arrival of the computerized catalog record—a development that would revolutionize reference search and retrieval.

When President Gerald R. Ford nominated Daniel Boorstin as Librarian of Congress on June 20, 1975, the Library experienced a reprise of the controversy surrounding the MacLeish nomination. The American Library Association again protested the naming of an individual without a library degree to the position. Despite the opposition Dr. Boorstin, like MacLeish, was confirmed by the Senate. He took office on November 12, 1975, the twelfth in the procession of Librarians of Congress.

The parallels between the tenures of Boorstin and MacLeish extend beyond the facts of their appointments. Both men were scholars and authors; both initiated sweeping changes in the Library's organization. Perhaps most importantly, both shared a vision of the Library as the instrument of the American people, MacLeish referring to "the reference library of the people" and Boorstin to "the People's Library."

OPENING UP—REACHING OUT

The philosophy of the Boorstin years might be described in one word, *openness*. In keeping with his emphasis on the people's library, Dr. Boorstin decreed that the massive bronze doors leading into the Jefferson Building's Great Hall should be opened to the public. Since the Main Reading Room is immediately adjacent to the Great Hall, this opening led readers directly into the reading room.

At Dr. Boorstin's suggestion, the curtains screening the reading desks in the room were removed, and, as noted in his annual report, "the opening up of space immediately inside the west entrance made the general atmosphere more inviting." He commented further:

> The Main Reading Room is the focus of much of the Library's service to readers utilizing the general book collections and is the location from which many are referred to the special collections and facilities. This was the logical place, therefore, to start to make the readers' introduction to the Library smoother and more productive. . . . Additional staff members were assigned to the Main Reading Room to provide research guidance and assistance, particularly to those using the Library for the first time, and a number of new brochures were made available. A cataloger was assigned to a new work station to help readers use the card catalog. These and other improvements, formalized in May at a reception entitled "Openings," have been well received by the Library's users. The increase in the number of readers given reference assistance is one indication that the program has been successful in projecting the message that the Library staff is present to provide help (**11** 1977, p. 43.).

Unfortunately the new policy of opening the doors also brought in the tourists, many of whom asserted what they believed to be their taxpayers' right to stroll through the room and look at the readers. The patience of the reference librarians often wore thin as they tried tactfully to direct the visitors to the observation gallery. Even from the gallery the sightseers persisted in shooting flash pictures, a practice that violated the rules and disturbed researchers below.

The new emphasis on openness extended beyond the Library's buildings to new programs of exchange with other libraries. While the reference staff had for many years answered ques-

FOUR LIBRARIANS OF CONGRESS GATHERED ON OCTOBER 2, 1979, TO CELEBRATE
THE FORTIETH ANNIVERSARY OF ARCHIBALD MACLEISH'S APPOINTMENT AS LIBRARIAN.
LEFT TO RIGHT: LUTHER EVANS, ARCHIBALD MACLEISH, DANIEL J. BOORSTIN,
AND L. QUINCY MUMFORD. LC-USP6-8435-M, FRAME 16A

tions directed to the Library by telephone and mail, under Dr. Boorstin the Library mounted two programs to enlist the cooperation of other American libraries in channeling appropriate reference inquiries to the Library of Congress and, in turn, answering questions from the Library on a local or state level. The first program is described in the General Reference and Bibliography Division report for 1976: "Public Reference laid plans and secured the cooperation of five library networks in a pilot project for a National Telephone Reference Service" (p. 8). The five networks represented public and academic libraries in the major regions of the United States. The Library's Telephone Reference Unit provided them with reference information that could not be found with ease locally.

The Congress declined to appropriate funds for an expansion of the service beyond the pilot stage, which ran from July 12 to September 1976, but a second cooperative reference program fared better. The Library sponsored the first Cooperative Reference Exchange with the Western Council of State Librarians in September 1981. The second exchange a year later included southern and eastern state library agencies. A total of forty-one states participated.

These week-long seminars were designed by Ellen Z. Hahn, the new chief of the General Reading Rooms Division, to develop closer ties between state library and Library of Congress reference staffs and to improve access to their respective services and resources. Her efforts to procure the cooperation of state librarians led directly to the establishment of a correspondence referral program that flourished and is still administered by the division.

Another hallmark of the Boorstin years was the movement of Library staff across division and even department lines to improve service to readers. The participation of Main Reading Room staff in Library-wide activities as well as their success in projecting Dr. Boorstin's message that "the Library staff is present to provide help," is shown in a report of Dr. Edward MacConomy, acting chief of the General Reference and Bibliography Division. Detailing the results of a reader survey conducted by the Librarian's Task Force on Goals, Organization, and Planning, he described proudly how,

> With the same size staff as two years ago, the reference librarians managed to offer quality assistance despite a serious depletion in ranks caused by absence at computer terminal training and at meetings of the Task Force subcommittees and the Committee on GR&B Organization. Indeed, in the reader survey taken almost at the height of the reader, meeting, and training frenzy, six in ten readers who had consulted the reference librarians in the MRR [Main Reading Room], our busiest room, found them "very helpful"; another three in ten found them helpful, and only one in thirty found them unhelpful or very unhelpful (**IOA** 1976).

TIME FOR REORGANIZATION

By 1978, the reorganization planned by Dr. Boorstin was in place. The former Reader Services Department was now called Research Services, administered by Donald C. Curran, Acting Assistant Librarian. Ellen Z. Hahn became chief of what was renamed the General Reading Rooms Division (GRR).

The new division was formed largely from elements of the disbanded General Reference and Bibliography Division and the Stack and Reader Division. It now comprised the Main Reading Room, the Thomas Jefferson Reading Room, the Local History and Genealogy Reading Room and the Microform Reading Room, the special study facilities, and three reference functions—telephone inquiry, reference correspondence, bibliography functions. The Public Reference Section was split into four units—Main Reading Room, Thomas Jefferson Reading Room, Telephone Inquiry, and Automation and Reference Collections. Finally, the staff of the Research Guidance Office (RGO), formerly attached to the office of the director of the Reader Services Department, was transferred to the Main Reading Room section.

The addition of the RGO staff gave impetus to the division's plan for staff rotation. The object was to rotate reference staff among a number of service points in the reading rooms sections and the other offices. A staff committee recommended that the rotation plan cover the work stations, allow flexibility in scheduling, and provide maximum opportunities for personal and professional staff development. "By year's end reference librarians were staffing the Research Guidance Office, the Issue Desk, Alcoves 4 and 5, and the Computer Catalog Center on an experimental basis to determine the most effective way to serve the variety of reader needs expressed at each location, as well as to maximize the wealth of expertise available among the staff" (**10B** 1978 p. 3).

As is the way of many experiments, the trial became the practice. For a glimpse of how the staff coped with constant motion in the 1980s, a report from the front lines, first published in Mississippi Libraries, summer 1980, is reprinted below (see pages 52–53).

During the eighties, Main Reading Room reference librarians also compiled finding aids, published bibliographies and books in their subject fields, lectured, gave speeches at library schools, and attended professional meetings. In 1984, the division established a new public training program for users of the Library's online systems, presented in the Library's Automation Orientation Center. More than a thousand users and staff received training that year. The program continues to be popular with the public, and Main Reading Room librarians participate heavily in teaching the courses.

In a spirit of intralibrary cooperation, Main Reading Room staff members were joined by reference librarians from science and loan divisions, who helped to staff the Computer Catalog Center and the Research Guidance Office. An experimental cooperative project cutting across department lines enlisted subject catalogers in helping readers to search the Main Card Catalog. The Catalog Assistance Program was followed some years later by another cooperative effort, this time with descriptive catalogers who staffed the Computer Catalog Center together with Main Reading Room reference staff.

THE POWER OF THE MACHINE: A MIXED BLESSING

An unscientific but appreciated evaluation of the Main Reading Room reference librarians was included in a division report written in 1975 by chief Robert Land. As he related: "A researcher indoctrinating another in the use of the Library paused at the MRR reference desks and was overheard making the accurate observation that 'This is one of the most valuable parts of the Library. These people can answer almost any question you can think of'" (**10A** 1975, p. 2). If this flattering assessment were true in the days before automation, how much truer must it be today when the reference staff benefits by the advances made in the Library's use of computers?

In 1945 Dr. Evans looked forward to the day when Vannevar Bush's "memex" or other "cheap complex device of great reliability" was available. Thirty years later, when Dr. Boorstin took office, he could marvel at how far we had traveled.

Within the last century, however, and especially within the last few decades, this Library has come to bear vivid witness, in quite new ways, to the power of the Machine. . . . The output of printing presses has been multiplying. The items which our Library receives in a single day are more than five times the whole number of volumes purchased from Thomas Jefferson in 1815.

Now, by a lucky coincidence, the electronic computer makes it possible for us to keep track of our gargantuan collections. Dr. Mumford, my distinguished predecessor . . . ushered our great

Library into the age of automation, and so has helped save us from being buried under our own treasures (**13** November 21, 1975, p. 460).

Not only did the computer open up avenues for control of our "gargantuan collections," it added a powerful reference tool to the librarians' armory by instituting online bibliographic search in the Reference Department. In April 1975 the first computer terminal for public use in the Library of Congress was installed in the Science Reading Room in the Science and Technology Division. Using the SCORPIO programs (developed for the Congressional Research Service), the terminal provided access by author, title, subject, LC classification number, or card number to approximately ninety-thousand English-language monographs in the fields of science and technology selected from the Library's MARC data base. "This system is a pilot application that the Reference Department hopes will yield useful clues about possible future public use of on-line computer terminals on a much larger scale" (**11** 1975, p. 50).

Automation came to the Main Reading Room modestly enough in May 1976 with the installation of one terminal for both public and staff use on an adjacent deck. In 1977, computer services were expanded and made more accessible to both readers and staff.

> Most apparent to the public is the new Computer Catalog Center in the Main Catalog area, where six terminals, two with printout capability, were grouped as an addition to the even larger number available in the reading rooms. In the center, staff members are present during much of the workday to train new users. The facility was received enthusiastically by patrons. Problems relative to reliability and response time have been minimized by the immediate accessibility of the

LIBRARY OF CONGRESS:
A WEEK'S WORTH OF QUESTIONS

BY JUDITH FARLEY
A SENIOR REFERENCE LIBRARIAN IN THE MAIN READING
ROOM
(REPRINTED FROM *MISSISSIPPI LIBRARIES*, SUMMER 1980)

MONDAY. Since our staff of 14 librarians covers five reference stations in the Main Reading Room, the master schedule is our most basic reference tool. Just before the doors open at 8:30, I check the schedule to see which station I've drawn first. The Research Guidance Office (RGO) located directly inside the reading room's entrance from the Great Hall, offers many readers their initial contact with a reference librarian. In the two hours I'm stationed here, I suggest appropriate sources, subject headings, and relevant materials in custodial divisions to researchers needing information on such varied topics as commercial finance companies, local histories of parishes in Norway and women's work in World War I (listed, of course, under European War, 1914–1918). I also make referrals, answer many tourists' questions, explain how to order books from the stacks, and suggest, at the request of a newly engaged couple, "a romantic, elegant restaurant to celebrate in."

As I offer congratulations, my replacement arrives at RGO, which means I now move on to the alcoves. Usually three librarians are stationed here, in the heart of the rooms 45,000 volumes, so we can work more intensely with readers. Just now a woman wants help in compiling a legislative history of the Voting Rights Act. This entails finding the original bill, locating the floor debates in the *Congressional Record,* tracing the reports in the *U.S. Serial Set,* tracking down the hearings, and finally, finding the law in the *Statutes-at-Large.*

In contrast the next request I field is simple, "How do you use *Reader's Guide to Periodical Literature?*" Our patrons are such a varied group, of such differing ages, educational levels, interests, and degrees of familiarity with libraries, that working here provides constant challenges and continual surprises.

Although dealing directly with the public forms the biggest part of my day, after lunch I'm scheduled for two hours away from the public desk. I use the time to answer a letter from a man in Belgium who wants to know, "quite simply," as he writes with touching faith in the Library, whether Anne Bradstreet's poem, "The Four Ages of Man" is an analogue of the concept of time inherent in Spenser's "The Shepherdes Calendar." Quite simply, the answer is no, but I sense this will not do and struggle with an explanation of the poem.

TUESDAY. I report to work this morning in the Library's Training Office to participate in a workshop on disruptive readers. Because of the movement in the mental health care field to "mainstream" into society mental patients formerly institutionalized, LC, like other urban libraries, faces a continuing problem with disturbed readers. Today's workshop, the result of a union-management agreement, is for public service personnel—special police, librarians, and others. It includes speakers from the Psychiatric Institute (a private mental health center in Washington), the Library's General Counsel's Office, and the Protective Services Office. It seems to me that the workshops are creating a support system among our public staff and the administration; I come away much encouraged and better prepared to face the occasional disturbed reader.

WEDNESDAY. My day off, since I work this coming Saturday. I like shopping during the week when the stores are less crowded, but I sometimes feel I'm being mistaken for a member of the leisured class.

THURSDAY. "No sir, you didn't break the terminal; the computer is just processing your command," I reassure a nervous reader in the Computer Catalog Center. At this station, we teach patrons how to use the Library of Congress Information System, which gives access to the online catalog, and our internal data bases. It's always interesting to see the variety of patron responses to the computer; enthusiastic or adamantly opposed, eager or hesitant, few users are indifferent to the new technology. At times, however, after two hours of repeating the simple commands used in the system, I dread the arrival of January 2, 1981, when we close the card catalog.

But later in the day while working in the alcoves, I'm impressed all over again at the computer's usefulness (and at my colleague's ingenuity), as I watch Tom conduct a reference interview with a deaf reader by typing questions and answers on a terminal screen. Since both librarian and reader are good typists, the transaction goes quickly and satisfactorily for both parties.

FRIDAY. Another chance to sleep late, since I'm on the 1 to 9:30 P.M. shift today. Eating a leisurely breakfast is fine, but working these hours means that supper is taken at 4 P.M. So much for elegant dining. But there are advantages to evening duty. Although only three librarians are working, the pace usually slows after 7 o'clock sufficiently so that I can write reference letters, compile the weekly statistics for the section, or recommend acquisitions in my subject specialty, British literature. On the other hand, the telephone inquiry section closes at 5, and all calls are then answered in the reading room. Since the assistance we can offer by phone is rather limited, I find it less satisfying than reference work by letter or in person. Of course, on Friday nights we're more apt to get telephone calls from people who begin, "We're having a party and want to settle a bet . . ."

SATURDAY. Surveying the reading room from my favorite stations, the Central Desk in the middle of the room, I brace myself for a busy day; it's only 10 o'clock and I've already recorded 200 people on the digital counter. This location is our circulation desk where readers present call slips, and books arrive for delivery to patron's seats. The librarians share this station with the Collections Management staff, who are responsible for book service. Because readers rarely make a distinction between the two staffs and because the location is highly visible, the stream of readers is heavy. I often feel like a policewoman (or at least a crossing guard) when directing traffic up to the Law Library or over to the Thomas Jefferson Building, or explaining where the cafeteria is ("On the cellar level, which is below the basement or street floor—we're on the first floor.")

Directly opposite the Central Desk the card catalog begins. Containing about 17,000,000 cards, it continues in the middle room, the hall, and Room 154. I've yet to think of a tactful answer to the innocent questions, "Where's the card catalog?" To say, "Right here," seems obvious, while "It's all around you" sounds a bit ominous, and "Oh, it's easy to miss," although comforting, isn't really true. But one question asked frequently is easy to answer. Standing in the center of this impressive room, looking at the marble walls, the gold and stucco dome, and the rich wood fittings, readers often ask,"What's it like to work in such a beautiful room?" and I answer, "It's great."

REFERENCE LIBRARIAN THOMAS MANN AT THE CENTRAL DESK COMPLETING THE CIRCLE
BETWEEN READER AND CATALOG, CA. 1985. LC-USP6-9814, FRAME 36

card catalog, and valuable experience is being gained which will be needed when the card catalog is closed and computer terminals replace manual files in the years to come (**11** 1977, p. 43).

By 1981, it was evident that the "pilot application" described in the 1975 annual report was a permanent fixture, whose only change would be growth and increased sophistication. The nature of reference work was transformed forever by the presence of the computer. By 1981, another prediction had come true—the card catalog was "frozen." After December 31, 1980, no new cards would ever be added to it. The computer was the only searchable book file for items acquired after that date. The Librarian's report for 1981 noted:

> With the January closing of the Main Card Catalog, computer terminals have become the preferred means of access to current catalog information. Because of the growing use of computer terminals, the Computer Catalog Center, located behind the Main Reading Room, was expanded in February from six to eighteen terminals, most with associated printers. Two reference librarians are now on duty in the expanded center during peak hours and provide training for new users and some instruction in advanced techniques for those experienced in computer searching (**11** 1981, p. 81).

Although widely hailed for speed of search and ease of retrieval, automated book files were not universally regarded as the only catalogs readers would ever need. More than one critic pointed out that card catalogs and online catalogs should coexist, for each one could do things that the other could not. Stanley Goldberg, of the Smithsonian Institution, a frequent researcher at the Library of Congress, asserted that "The structure of the card catalog did not emerge overnight. Its architecture was undoubtedly shaped by decades of the shared experience of users, reference librarians and catalogers. The computer catalog in the Library of Congress is now a poor substitute for the card catalog for those of us using the catalog as a research tool" (**6** p 32).

The card catalog found other strong supporters on the reference staff itself, among them Dr. Thomas Mann, a reference specialist from the Main Reading Room. Fearing the disposal of the cards once they had been entered into a retrospective online file and also photographed on microfilm, he wrote several memos that described the unsatisfactory nature of the retrospective online file (PREMARC). He warned that many old and valuable materials were filed in PREMARC under obsolete subject headings which had been updated in the card catalog.

> For example, an aviation historian who searches under the proper term "Airplanes" in the database will get 136 postings—but he will miss 4,490 books posted under the incorrect heading "Aeroplanes." This is the obsolete heading used by the Library in the early years of the century. All of the cards in the MCat [Main Card Catalog] under "Aeroplanes" were changed decades ago to the current term "Airplanes"; but the MCat was not used for creating PREMARC. Instead PREMARC was created from a different catalog called the Shelflist, which has accurate authors, titles, and call numbers—but not accurate subject headings. The Shelflist retains all of the old and obsolete headings used from the first 80 years of LC cataloging (**10** memo, June 11, 1985).

Thus he and others, including the Librarian of Congress, concluded that the card catalog must be retained. Reliable searching for old material was simply not practical without it.

UNREST IN THE READING ROOM

Patterns of service in the Main Reading Room remained generally calm until March 1986, when implementation of the Gramm-Rudman-Hollings Balanced Budget and Emergency Deficit Control Act cut Library funds and led to reductions in force and early closing hours. The reading room was closed on Sundays and on every evening except Wednesday. These reductions affected service to readers, a few of whom complained noisily. Dr. Boorstin's annual report explained that:

> a group calling itself "Books Not Bombs" took it upon itself to attack the President's budget by, among other things, staging a sit-in in the Main Reading Room, as a protest to the Library's reduced hours. The group, in effect, was determined to "keep the reading room open" beyond its new 5:30 P.M. closing time. The Library took no action the first two nights, hoping that the demonstration, which lasted until the former closing time of 9:30 P.M., would make its point and discontinue. It did not. On the third night of the sit-in, the Library, pursuant to proper police procedures, began arresting those who remained after Library officers gave the proper warnings and time to respond. In all, eighteen arrests were made . . . (II 1986, p. 4).

By July funds had been made available from a supplemental appropriations bill which allowed the Library to restore reading room hours. Normal hours resumed on July 10, "four months to the day after their curtailment." Musing on the impact of the disruption, the Librarian wrote that,

> According to Kierkegaard, life can only be understood backwards, but it must be lived forwards. Library staff members, coping with exasperated and disruptive readers in mid-March did not know that within four months this particular problem would be solved, though it might have made things easier if they had. Nevertheless, there was permanent damage done in 1986 to the department programs, and permanent scars remain (II 1986, p. 67).

Today scars inflicted in 1986 have faded. Nevertheless readers at the time had spoken decisively about how important their reading room and its complement of services were to them.

CLOSED FOR RENOVATION

The Librarian was optimistic in describing plans for temporary closing of the Main Reading Room. "The inevitable day approached when the Main Reading Room, for the past ninety years the principal jewel in the Library's crown, would be affected by renovation and restoration plans. After some delays, that date was identified as December 9, 1987. Much planning went into mitigating the impact of that closing, estimated to last one calendar year" (II 1987, p. 80).

Reading room restoration was part of an overall rejuvenation of the Thomas Jefferson Building and the John Adams Building initiated and implemented by Dr. Boorstin. By 1987 the luster of the "principal jewel" had dimmed sadly. That renovation was necessary was obvious; that it would take more than three years to complete, no one anticipated.

The inevitable day also approached when Dr. Boorstin would add the title "emeritus" to his office, bringing to an end twelve years of visionary and forceful leadership. The year 1987 saw the closing of both the reading room and the Boorstin era, and it brought the expectations of a new beginning under Dr. James Billington and the promise of new splendor for the Main Reading Room.

L ike his distinguished predecessors, James H. Billington, the present Librarian of Congress, is a scholar and a man of letters. Like them, he has instituted a program of institutional reorganization. And like them, too, he envisions the Library as the instrument of a democratic nation. MacLeish called it "the reference library of the people," Boorstin, "the People's Library," and Billington, "the living encyclopedia of democracy."

Each Librarian builds on the strengths of his predecessors, but each one also leads the institution in new directions. The sense of new beginnings was strong as Dr. Billington took the oath of office as the thirteenth Librarian of Congress on September 14, 1987. Restoration and revival of the Library's physical fabric would be matched by the infusion of new ideas and a revitalization of its intellectual life.

At his induction, Dr. Billington said:

> I especially like that word *vital*: full of life. For libraries are today's living link between the record of yesterday and the possibilities of tomorrow. The Library of Congress is not just all these books and buildings, but the anguish, achievements, and aspirations of our forefathers living on here near the heart of our country. This Library's life blood is all those people who keep the rejuvenating flow of free inquiry circulating through our land: millions everywhere who benefit from these collections, thousands on the staff who keep them healthy, and the variety of users who come here to blend memory with desire into hope: the researcher seeking truth, the artist creating beauty, and the legislator devising the good (**13** vol. 46, September 21, 1987, p. 406).

FIRST PRIORITY—REORGANIZATION

The new Librarian hit the ground running and staff scrambled to keep up with him. Almost immediately he began planning for reorganization. To head his Management and Planning (MAP) Committee, he tapped Ellen Hahn, chief of the General Reading Rooms Division and Winston Tabb, a former division administrator. He also retained a private consulting firm to ensure creative planning. Reading room staff participated in MAP's coffee hours and discussions, writing memos and making presentations for their favorite issues.

After a year of planning, the second phase of reorganization began. Staff were sent scrambling to participate in work modules designed to implement the initial decisions—emphasis on collections and participatory management. When the dust settled, the reorganized Library structure featured new offices such as Cultural Affairs and Special Projects. The traditional responsibilities of the Library were represented by two new departments, Collections Services and Constituent Services.

Within Constituent Services the General Reading Rooms Division began planning its own reorganization. Moving away from the former organizational design that assigned librarians to sections based on their work location (for instance, Main Reading Room Section or Social Science Reading Room Section) the new plan called for placing librarians, according to their reference specialties, into subject-oriented teams. History, Arts and Humanities, Social Sciences, Genealogy, and Business teams were created to emphasize the development of the collections and to stimulate creative publication in subject areas. All of the teams, except Genealogy and Business, would serve in the Main Reading Room on its reopening.

By the end of 1987, the users evoked so poetically in Dr. Billington's remarks would have one less reading room in which to pursue their ends, whether truth, beauty, or the good. The half million visitors who viewed the Main Reading Room from the gallery and the 199,000 researchers who used its facilities in 1987 would be the last members of the public to see it for a considerable time.

There was no interruption in public service. At five o'clock on closing day, December 9, the librarians on duty that evening walked across the street to report for work in the Social Science Reading Room of the Adams Building. It was not, of course, an easy transition. Two years of careful planning and intensive effort by the administrators of the General Reading Rooms Division and the Collections Management Division lay behind the smooth transfer of public service from one building to the other.

Suzanne Thorin, acting chief of the General Reading Rooms Division, explained that "The plan . . . designated how and when the following would be moved: 1) MRR reference collections (45,000 volumes); 2) the card catalogs, the largest being the Main Catalog with 22,184 drawers; 3) terminals, printers, and photocopy machines; 4) 1,210 desk and shelf holders; 5) all reference functions; and 6) the staff itself. In addition, signage and numerous publications were prepared. Without a doubt, every staff member assisted in some way to make the transition smooth" (IOB 1988, p. 4). To facilitate service, a renovated Center Room on the fifth floor of the Adams Building containing a Computer Catalog Center with sixteen work stations, a book service desk, and a photocopy center, opened simultaneously with the closing of the Main Reading Room.

Knowing that the Main Reading Room closing would result in the loss of two hundred seats for readers, the administration planned to accommodate the overflow crowds in the pavilion of the Local History and Genealogy Reading Room and to open the European and Hispanic reading rooms on Saturdays and the Manuscript Reading Room on Sundays. In fact, as Ms. Thorin later noted, "The number of readers that we anticipated would use the Local History and Genealogy Reading Room for general library materials did not materialize, and therefore we moved some staff to the Social Science Reading Room, which had become a very busy hub" (IOB 1988, p.5).

Unexpected problems were solved and fine-tuning took place in the first two months after the closing. Staff and supervisors spent months trying to make conditions in the Adams Building hospitable to readers. Deck 7, where the Main Card Catalog, the Main Reading Room Reference Collection, and the telephone and city directories were moved, suffered from a lack of air circulation, improper lighting, and cramped space. Signs, some table space for readers, and hall lights were added, and staff prepared a detailed map of the area, which improved service and morale. Card drawers were frequently found out of place because of unclear labeling, which would be corrected when the catalog was moved back to the Jefferson Building. The reference desk in the Social Science Reading Room was too small to accommodate either staff or the materials they needed to work with.

Although staff and readers did adjust gracefully to unfamiliar quarters and awkward conditions, the physical dislocation incurred some psychic discomfort. Librarians missed the Main Reading Room as they would have missed an old and valued friend.

STAFF ACTIVITIES

Closing the Main Reading Room made possible the amalgamation of two reading room staffs into one. This in turn meant more time for staff to participate in many important Library-wide

ALMOST FULL CIRCLE. . . . WIRING IS STILL EXPOSED AND TABLE LAMPS STILL DRAPED WITH PLASTIC SHEETS, BUT THIS VIEW CAPTURES THE GLORY OF THE RESTORED MAIN READING ROOM. (PHOTOGRAPH BY REID BAKER, MARCH 21, 1991.)

activities which have, or will have, great impact on service to readers. Such activities included automation planning at various levels and for different purposes.

Improvements in the Library's automation capacities were pursued by the General Reading Rooms Division and by several reading room staff members who worked with the automation offices to make systems user friendly and to instruct readers in the use of online search facilities. Recognizing that it was not practical to staff expanded computer centers with librarians whose role was to train the public in the use of command-driven search systems, division specialists played a major role in the design of ACCESS, a microcomputer-based touch-screen program that will enable beginning searchers to retrieve information from the MUMS and SCORPIO files without training or assistance from reference librarians.

In helping Dr. Billington keep his pledge to share the Library's riches with the American people, a number of Main Reading Room librarians have been heavily involved with two bibliographic outreach pilots, both coordinated and administered by division chief Suzanne Thorin. The Remote Online User Pilot (ROLLUP) was designed to provide direct dial-up access to the Library's computer catalogs. The book files as well as the bibliographic, congressional bill status, copyright, and referral information files could be searched at fourteen library test sites around the country.

The second pilot, called LC DIRECT, is intended to test the feasibility of offering access to the Library's online systems to the state library agencies on a subscription basis. Since these agencies are mandated to meet the information needs of the state legislatures and to facilitate the development and extension of statewide library services, they are the logical organizations through which the Library of Congress can disseminate its resources to the largest number of citizens in the most efficient and cost-effective method. These pilots are concrete examples of the Librarian's desire to harness electronic technologies to create "an electronic Library without walls," so that the collections of the Library of Congress can be used by people all across the country.

The next decade is proving to be an exciting time for the Library and its staff. Dr. Billington has observed that "There are frontiers to be explored in terms of the new technologies, for sharing . . . some of the content of this great Library. . . . There are new technologies emerging, offering opportunities which may even be obligations. We may find new ways to share some of the richness of this repository of national memory" (**13** October 26, 1987, p. 459, 462).

MAIN READING ROOM REOPENED

In light of the Librarian's interest in extending the Library's walls metaphorically, it is felicitous to think that it has also fallen to him to complete the physical restoration of the Jefferson and Adams buildings begun by Dr. Boorstin, and that it will be his pleasure to preside over the reopening of the Main Reading Room. The opening will bring the reading room full circle to the beginning of a new century of service and will mark the first in a number of celebrations that will climax, in the year 2000, with the two hundredth birthday of the Library itself.

In the theatrical sense, the Main Reading Room has been dark for more than three years as workmen have sought to repair the leaks in the roof and the other ravages of time. They have been engaged in cleaning the marble, restoring the gilt, moving the card cases, replacing the carpets, and installing the cables that will bring in modern computer technology. These and countless other tasks have been necessary for full renovation.

As the Main Reading Room reopens its doors, the circles of service between librarian and reader are turning again in their natural home. The Main Reading Room has come full circle, ready to enter a third century of service to Congress and the nation.

1.
Adams, James Truslow, 1878–1949.
 The epic of America / by James Truslow Adams. — Boston : Little, Brown, 1931. — viii p., 2 leaves, [3]–433 p. : ill.
 E178.A258

2.
Angle, Paul McClelland, 1900–
 The Library of Congress : an account, historical and descriptive. — Kingsport, Tenn. : Printed by the Kingsport Press, 1948. — 77 p.
 Z733.U6A55

3.
Bishop, William Warner, 1871–1955.
 The Library of Congress, 1907–1915. — In Library quarterly. — Vol. 18 (Jan. 1948) ; p. 7–13.
 Z671.L713

4.
Clapp, Verner W.
 Three ages of reference work. — In Special libraries. — Vol. 57 (July/Aug. 1966) ; p. 379–384.
 Z671.S72

5.
Cole, John Y., 1940–
 For Congress and the Nation : a chronological history of the Library of Congress through 1975. — Washington : Library of Congress, 1979. — xiii, 196 p. : ill.
 Z733.U6C565
 Bibliography: p. 177–179.

6.
Goldberg, Stanley.
 Catalog conundrums : a user's view. — In Automation at the Library of Congress : inside views / edited by Suzanne E. Thorin. — Washington : Library of Congress Professional Association, 1986. — p. 30–33.
 Z733.U6A85 1986

7.
Goodrum, Charles A.
 Computerization at the Library of Congress : the first twenty years / by Charles Goodrum and Helen Dalrymple. — In Automation at the Library of Congress : inside views / edited by Suzanne E. Thorin. — Washington : Library of Congress Professional Association, 1986. — p. 1–3.
 Z733.U6A85 1986

8.
Goodrum, Charles A.
 The Library of Congress / Charles A. Goodrum and Helen W. Dalrymple. — Boulder, Colo. : Westview Press, 1982. — ix, 337 p. : ill. — (Westview library of federal departments, agencies, and system.)
 Z733.U6G67 1982
 Bibliography: p. 317–322.

9.
Hilker, Helen-Anne.
 Ten First Street, Southeast : Congress builds a library, 1886–1897 : an exhibition in the Great Hall and on the second floor of the Thomas Jefferson Building, Library of Congress from December 23, 1980, to December 7, 1981 / Helen-Anne Hilker. — 2nd ed. — Washington : Library of Congress, 1982. — iii, 102 p. : ill.
 Z679.2.U54H54 1982
 Includes bibliographical references.

10.
Library of Congress.
 Library of Congress Archives. Manuscript Division. Library of Congress. — Washington, D.C.
 A. General Reference and Bibliography Division annual reports.
 B. General Reading Rooms Division annual reports.

11.
Library of Congress.
   Report of the Librarian of Congress [annual report]. — (1865/1866)-   . — Washington : U.S. Govt. Print Off., 1866–

   Z733.U57A
   Reporting year may vary.
   Title varies slightly.

12.
   The Library of Congress [microform] : a documentary history / edited by John Y. Cole. — Bethesda, Md. : CIS Academic Editions, c1987. — 594 microfiches : negative ; 11 x 15 cm.
         Microfiche 87/974 (z) LTMiCRR MT
   Accompanied by a printed guide to the microfiche collection (micrr guide no. 171) edited by John Y. Cole, with a foreword by Daniel J. Boorstin. Guide includes bibliographies and indexes.

13.
   Library of Congress information bulletin. — Vol. 31, no. 1 (Jan. 1990)-   . — [Washington] : The Library, [1972–

   Z733.U5716
   Weekly, Jan. 1972–Dec. 1989.
   Biweekly, Jan. 1990.

14.
MacLeish, Archibald.
   The reorganization of the Library of Congress, 1939–44. — In Library quarterly. — Vol. 14 (Oct. 1944) ; p. 277–315.
   Z671.L713

15.
Mearns, David Chambers, 1889–
   The story up to now : the Library of Congress, 1800–1946. — Washington : [U.S. Govt. Print. Off.], 1947. — iii, 226 p. : ill.
   Z773.U6M45
   Reprinted from the Annual report of the Librarian of Congress for the fiscal year ending June 30, 1946, with the addition of illustrations and a slight revision of text.
   Reprinted in Boston by Gregg Press in 1972.

16.
Mohrhardt, Foster E.
   Dr. William Warner Bishop : our first international librarian. — In An American library history reader : contributions to library literature / [compiled by John David Marshall]. — Hamden, Conn. : Shoe String Press, 1961 [c1960] — p. 347.

17.
Morrisey, Marlene.
   Verner W. Clapp : 1901–1972. — In LCPA newsletter. — Vol. 3 (July/Aug. 1972) ; p. 7.
   Z733.W3114

18.
Sittig, William J.
   Luther Evans : man for a new age. — In Librarians of Congress, 1802–1974. — Washington : Library of Congress, 1977. — p. 220–237.

   Z720.A4L52
   Bibliographical references included in "Notes" (p. 237).

19.
Scott, Edith.
   J. C. M. Hanson and his contribution to twentieth-century cataloging. — 1970. — 2 v. (iv, 695 leaves).

   Z720.H26S35
   Thesis—University of Chicago.
   Bibliography: leaves 669–695.

20.
Small, Herbert.
   Handbook of the new Library of Congress, compiled by Herbert Small; with essays on the architecture, sculpture and painting, by Charles Caffin, and on the function of a national library, by Ainsworth R. Spofford. — Boston : Curtis & Cameron, 1899. — 3 leaves, 128 p. : ill., front., plan.
   Reprinted in Washington by Library of Congress Professional Association in 1976
   Z733.U58S63 1899

21.
United States. Library of Congress.
   Herbert Putnam, 1861–1955: a memorial tribute. — Washington : [The Library], 1956. — vii, 94 p.

   Z720.P9U52

22.
Wells, H. G. (Herbert George), 1866–1946.
   The future in America : a search after realities / by H. G. Wells. — New York and London : Harper & brothers, 1906. — 4 leaves, 259 p. : ill., front., plates.

   E168.W45

COMPILED BY KAREN BELANGER

Works issued by the Government Printing Office may be available at government depository libraries. Other works, including periodical articles, should be available at large public or university libraries.

Benco, Nancy.
Archibald MacLeish : the poet librarian. — In Librarians of Congress, 1802–1974. — Washington : Library of Congress, 1977. — p. 203–219.
Z720.A4L52
Government Printing Office, Superintendent of Documents, depository item.

Boorstin, Daniel J. (Daniel Joseph), 1914–
The republic of letters : Librarian of Congress Daniel J. Boorstin on books, reading, and libraries, 1975–1987 / edited by John Y. Cole. — Washington : Library of Congress, 1989.
Z1003.B735 1989

Broderick, John C.
John Russell Young : the internationalist as librarian. — In Librarians of Congress, 1802–1974. — Washington : Library of Congress, 1977. — p. 145–175.
Z720.A4L52
Government Printing Office, Superintendent of Documents, depository item.

Cole, John Y.
Ainsworth Rand Spofford : the valiant and persistent Librarian of Congress. — In Librarians of Congress, 1802–1974. — Washington : Library of Congress, 1977. — p. 119–141.
Z720.A4L52
Government Printing Office, Superintendent of Documents, depository item.

Cole, John Y.
The Library of Congress and American scholarship, 1865–1939. — In Libraries and scholarly communication in the United States : the historical dimension / edited by Phyllis Dain and John Y. Cole. — New York : Greenwood Press, 1990. — p. 45–61.
Z675.R45L53 1990

Cole, John Y.
Studying the Library of Congress : resources and research opportunities. — In Libraries & culture. — Vol. 24 (summer 1989) ; p. 357–366.
Z671.J67

Goodrum, Charles A.
Treasures of the Library of Congress / Charles A. Goodrum ; photography by Michael Freeman and Jonathan Wallen. — Rev. and expanded ed. — New York : H. N. Abrams, 1991. — 344 p. — ill. (some col.)
Z733.U58G66 1991

Gurney, Gene.
The Library of Congress : a picture story of the world's largest library / Gene Gurney & Nick Apple ; with special photography by Joseph Walters and Harold Wise. — New, updated, rev. ed., 1st rev. ed. — New York : Crown Publishers, c1981. — ix, 180 p. : ill.
Z733.U6 G86 1981

Lacy, Dan.
The Library of Congress : a sesquicentenary review. — In Library quarterly. — Vol. 20 (July and Oct. 1950) ; p. 157–179, 235–258.

Library of Congress.
Guide to the Library of Congress. — Washington : Library of Congress, 1982. — 119 p. : ill.
Z733.U6L45 1982
Written by Charles A. Goodrum and Helen W. Dalrymple.
Concise description of the Library of Congress with color photographs.

Library of Congress.
Research collections in the information age : the Library of Congress looks to the future / views by Stephen E. Ostrow and Robert Zich ; edited by John Y. Cole. — Washington : The Library, 1990. — vi, 18 p. — (The Center for the Book viewpoint series ; no. 27)
Z733.U58L38 1990

MacLeish, Archibald, 1892–
Champion of a cause : essays and addresses on librarianship / compiled and with an introd. by Eva M. Goldschmidt. — Chicago : American Library Association, 1971. — xiv, 248 p.
Z665.M158
Includes bibliographical references.

Mearns, David C.
Herbert Putnam, librarian of the United States. — In An American library history reader : contributions to library literature / [compiled by John David Marshall]. — Hamden, Conn. : Shoe String Press, 1961 [c1960]. — p. 362–410.

Z731.M3

Pierson, Harriet Wheeler, 1874–
Rosemary : reminiscences of the Library of Congress / by Harriet Wheeler Pierson. — Washington, 1943. — 23 p.

Z733.U58P5

Providing reference assistance for machine-readable materials : the Library of Congress completes a one-year pilot / John Kimball, Jr., Suzanne Thorin, Linda Arret. — In Reference librarian. — No. 31 (fall/winter 1990) ; p. 31–38.

Z711.R444

Describes the Machine-Readable Collections Reading Room in its first year at the Library.

Putnam, Herbert.
The national library : some recent developments. — In ALA Bulletin. — Vol. 22 (Sept. 1928) ; p. 346–355.

Z673.A5B8

Putnam, Herbert.
The Library of Congress. — In Atlantic monthly. — Vol. 85 (Feb. 1900) ; p. 145–158.

AP2.A8

Rosenberg, Jane Aiken.
Foundation for service : the 1896 hearings on the Library of Congress. — In Journal of library history. — Vol 21 (winter 1986) ; p. 107–130.

Z671.J67

Rosenberg, Jane Aiken.
The Library of Congress and the professionalization of American librarianship, 1896–1939. — 1988.
Thesis (PH.D.) — University of Michigan.

Salamanca, Lucy.
Fortress of freedom : the story of the Library of Congress / by Lucy Salamanca ; with a foreword by Archibald MacLeish. — Philadelphia ; New York : J. B. Lippincott co., 1942. — 445 p. front., plates, ports.

Small, Herbert.
The Library of Congress : its architecture and decoration / by Herbert Small ; edited by Henry Hope Reed ; foreword by Daniel J. Boorstin ; preface by Arthur Ross ; introduction by Pierce Rice. — 1st ed. — New York : Norton, c1982. — 215 p., [16] p. of plates : ill. (some col.). — (The Classical America series in art and architecture)

Z733.U6S6 1982

Previous ed. published as Handbook of the New Library of Congress. 1901.

Thomison, Dennis.
FDR, the ALA, and Mr. MacLeish : the selection of a Librarian of Congress, 1939. — In Library quarterly. Vol. 42 (Oct. 1972) ; p. 390–398.

Z671.L713

Wiegand, Wayne A.
Herbert Putnam's appointment as Librarian of Congress. — In Library quarterly. Vol. 49 (July 1979) ; p. 255–282.

Z671.L713